"In her fantastic debut, Mennonite pastor Florer-Bixler guides readers through a slow, participatory reading of the Old Testament. . . . Florer-Bixler proves herself a challenging teacher and inspiring preacher. Her impressive exploration of Old Testament themes will be a blessing for Christians seeking intellectually grounded spiritual guidance."

—*Publishers Weekly* starred review

"*Fire by Night* encapsulates Melissa Florer-Bixler's delight of Scripture, ancient literature, and God. I found myself challenged as a theologian, inspired as a pastor, and in tears as a person of faith trying to make sense of it all. What makes *Fire by Night* such an important book is that it speaks to today's issues without being prescriptive, while beckoning each of us to take the risk of simply being God's beloved."

—Theresa S. Thames, associate dean of religious life and the chapel at Princeton University

"Melissa Florer-Bixler's words cut deep, deep, still deeper and yet too cleanly for anyone to misunderstand. *Fire by Night* rescues the Old Testament from antiseptic Christian pieties and places it squarely in the mess of human life. Her language is ripe but limned smooth and spare as bone. This is the work of a Holy Ghost preacher, words burning on the page."

—Timothy B. Tyson, author of *Blood Done Sign My Name*

"Read this book for revelations of God, visions of God refracted through people and stories from the Old Testament and Melissa Florer-Bixler's life. These pages are full of grace and wonder—images of God's love for us and the world."

—Isaac S. Villegas, pastor of Chapel Hill Mennonite Fellowship

"*Fire by Night* is a beautifully written, kind invitation to see the God of the Old Testament through both modern and past stories of oppressed peoples who know God as Deliverer. This book is a true gem, giving language to the space between God and us—a relationship of community and presence."

—Kaitlin Curtice, Potawatomi author and speaker

"Too often, I have read the Old Testament through furrowed brow; those ancient stories and the God they depict feel impossibly remote. But Melissa Florer-Bixler's quietly powerful book erased that distance, and I am now reading Scripture with a reawakened sense of gratitude and awe.

—Christie Purifoy, author of *Roots and Sky*

"What awaits you in these pages, deeply grounded in pastoral ministry, are not just encounters with Old Testament stories but contemporary stories of children, neighbors, birds, bread, friendship, and more. . . . Melissa Florer-Bixler is courageous enough to engage the strange world of the Old Testament with patience and to wrestle with it to come out with a blessing for today."

—Luke Powery, dean of Duke University Chapel, from foreword

"Melissa Florer-Bixler's *Fire by Night* is an invitation to sit with the tension and unravel the hope present in the Old Testament. With thorough analysis, testimony, and revelation, *Fire by Night* delivers a powerful approach to Scripture. A slow and rooted invitation into God's presence is what makes this book a companion piece for a deeper study of the Old Testament."

—Carolina Hinojosa-Cisneros, Tejana poet, writer, and speaker

"*Fire by Night* illuminates how the Old Testament is a beautiful gift for contemporary readers, despite how its ancient contents are often stereotyped as merely an embarrassing problem. Melissa Florer-Bixler is a trustworthy guide through the Hebrew Scriptures as she gracefully brings together the wisdom of biblical scholarship along with the practical concerns for faithfulness in our everyday life.

—Drew G. I. Hart, author of *Trouble I've Seen*

"This is a bold exploration of Scripture by a persistent and learned reader. Florer-Bixler does not give up on what the Bible actually says even when it frustrates her. Her essays are full of deep pastoral wisdom and exegetical insight. She is teaching us to read the Old Testament for our lives."

—Ellen F. Davis, professor of Bible and practical theology at Duke Divinity School

MELISSA
FLORER-BIXLER

fire
by
night

FINDING
GOD IN THE PAGES OF THE OLD
TESTAMENT

WITHDRAWN

Herald
PRESS

Harrisonburg, Virginia

Herald Press
PO Box 866, Harrisonburg, Virginia 22803
www.HeraldPress.com

Library of Congress Cataloging-in-Publication Data
Names: Florer-Bixler, Melissa, author.
Title: Fire by night : finding God in the pages of the Old Testament /
    Melissa Florer-Bixler.
Description: Harrisonburg : Herald Press, 2019. | Includes bibliographical
    references.
Identifiers: LCCN 2018035097| ISBN 9781513804187 (pbk. : alk. paper) | ISBN
    9781513804194 (hardcover : alk. paper)
Subjects: LCSH: God--Biblical teaching. | Bible. Old Testament--Criticism,
    interpretation, etc.
Classification: LCC BS1192.6 .F56 2019 | DDC 221.6--dc23 LC record available
at https://lccn.loc.gov/2018035097

FIRE BY NIGHT
© 2019 by Herald Press, Harrisonburg, Virginia 22803. 800-245-7894.
All rights reserved.
Library of Congress Control Number: 2018035097
International Standard Book Number: 978-1-5138-0418-7 (paperback);
    978-1-5138-0420-0 (ebook); 978-1-5138-0419-4 (hardcover)
Printed in United States of America
Cover and interior design by Reuben Graham

Unless otherwise noted, Scripture text is quoted, with permission, from the *New Revised Standard Version,* © 1989, Division of Christian Education of the National Council of Churches of Christ in the United States of America.

Portions of chapter 8 are reprinted with permission from the August 1, 2017 issue of the *Christian Century.* Copyright © 2017 by the *Christian Century.*

Portions of chapter 9 were adapted from "Waiting to Be Surprised" from the December 2017 issue of *The Mennonite* and are used here with permission.

23 22 21 20 19   10 9 8 7 6 5 4 3 2 1

God tastes like fire.
—Hans Hut

Contents

A PRAYER FOR READERS OF THE OLD TESTAMENT

Perhaps you do not know how much
    you need God
    to come as a woman in labor,
    a birthing spirit hovering over creation,
    holding within her the memory of you
    nursing at her breast

Or to surprise you in ordinary places,
    searching in the fields for sheep,
    uprooting his garden,
    keeping her bees,
    a bird roosting in a tree.

If you look closely as you walk,
    if you pay attention
    with your eye on the book and world,
    the blessing will be
    as near as dirt, as close as air—
    a sprouting tree,
    a rushing fountain.

And if you rage or fear, if tears are your bread
God is there in the middle of it—
    a steaming pot,
    a raging she-bear,
    a smoking kiln
    or perhaps fire.
Always fire.[1]

FOREWORD

There are many ways to read the sacred pages of Scripture. Historical, literary, philological, postcolonial, as well as form and redaction readings: these approaches to biblical interpretation attempt to make meaning out of the often strange world of the Bible. That world—with its different languages, cultures, contexts, worldviews, characters, and images—can seem like a twilight zone. Yet the church, especially preachers and teachers of Scripture, is called on to wrestle with and interpret that ancient biblical world for today's world. This calling takes courage, humility, patience, and wisdom. It is risky. When we approach a Bible passage for interpretation and wrestle with it for textual meaning, we may walk away with a limp. Interpreting Scripture is not for the fainthearted but for those who are seeking the Heart at the heart of life—God.

Pastor Melissa Florer-Bixler is courageous enough to engage the strange world of the Old Testament with patience and tõ wrestle with it to come out with a blessing for today.

Regardless of what Christians think of the Old Testament, it is part of the Christian canon. It cannot be ignored and should be interpreted for the life of the church. There is gore, glory, and grace in the pages of the Old Testament, and all of it has meaning for then and for now. Florer-Bixler recognizes that sometimes there are more questions than answers, especially when one encounters the fire of God. Manna, water, wind, clouds, and fire? These are not of human creation and have no simple answers, because God is not simple. The stories of the Old Testament and God cannot be controlled. They are free and will not be bound by our limited and frail interpretations. Yet we are called to interpret, to preach—for the life of the world and for our lives.

Although the Old Testament can seem strange and for-eign—*other*—we approach it to listen, to learn, to live, even to love. And in that brave encounter with the other, we may discover that we are more alike than different. We know Jobs, and we are Job. We know Miriams, and we are Miriam. We know Josephs, and we are Joseph. We know Rachels, and we are Rachel. The stories and lives of those in the past are not necessarily or always so different from our own. We hurt. We laugh. We cry. We dance. We get angry. We ask God questions. We have family problems. We go on journeys but are not quite sure of the destinations. We play with fire and sometimes get burned.

But if we never play—if we never risk the delight of engag-ing the Old Testament—we may never know the terrible beauty that is God. If we never wrestle with these sacred texts, we may never experience the blessing God has for us.

What awaits you in these pages, deeply grounded in pasto-ral ministry, are not just encounters with Old Testament stories but contemporary stories of children, neighbors, birds, bread, friendship, and more. The "more" is fire, because the "more" is God. Florer-Bixler is interested not just in textual meanings but in grappling with the meaning of God—who God is and what God does, then and now.

This book is about more than just the Bible. Ultimately, it is about God, an invitation to find the God of reckoning, neighbors, victims, memory, wanderers, darkness, wonder, birds, the vulnerable, the table, friendship, in the pages of the Old Testament.

And when you find God in the Bible, and find God even in this book, you will encounter a fire that will hopefully set you aflame for life and love. In that vein, may these pages cause you to burn.

—Luke A. Powery, dean of Duke University Chapel and associate professor of homiletics at Duke University

PREFACE

My homiletics professor at Princeton Theological Seminary impressed upon me the importance of naming "the elephant in the room" when preaching. To ignore the obvious questions raised by Scripture was a sure way to lose any interest in the Word proclaimed from the pulpit.

Over time this has been marginally good preaching advice. But his observation helped me realize that the Old Testament itself is a kind of "elephant in the room" in my religious tradition.

What do we, the church, do with these books that take up roughly three-quarters of the Christian Bible? How do we read these words written in a world so different from ours, stories that are both ruthless and filled with grace? And does our reading change when we remember that we share these stories with our Muslim and Jewish neighbors?

For what it's worth, this book will not provide an easy answer to these questions. I don't provide a hermeneutical key, a reading strategy to get you past the difficult bits of Old

Testament violence. I won't clear up the hard parts of our Scriptures by imposing Christian frameworks as the essential interpretive principle. Instead, I welcome you to read alongside me, looking at the world from the inside of the Old Testament, to see what happens and what we discover along the way. I invite you to follow after God as Israel followed through the dark, God as the fire lighting the way, ablaze in awe and fear, wonder and hope.

One metaphor for God in the Old Testament is fire. Unwieldy and uncontrollable, common and extraordinary, bringing life and death, at the same time a gift of life and a source of fear, making light and revealing hidden places, burning up and burning away. The Old Testament smells of smoke.

WHEN I CAME to the idea of writing about the Old Testament, Marilynne Robinson's book *Lila* came to mind. *Lila* is the third in an interconnected set of books about a small town in Iowa and the town's Congregationalist pastor, John Ames.

Lila is the story's main character: an unwanted, forgotten child born into white itinerant farm poverty, a hard life. She grows up, economically worthless and struggling to survive. But then Lila happens upon an unexpected friendship, stumbling into a small town and into the life of the older and learned Reverend Ames.

One night, wandering from town to town in search of work, Lila meanders into Reverend John Ames's church to get out of the rain. And it is there that Lila discovers the Bible. As she settles into life in the town of Gilead, she reads more of the book. Lila is especially taken by the prophecy of Ezekiel.

John Ames is anxious about Lila's fascination with the apocalyptic vision of Ezekiel. As a wise and learned man of the cloth, Ames endeavors to explain to Lila that the stories in the prophets, visions like those in Ezekiel, all the many-eyed angels and abominations and lions devouring humans—it's all allegory and poetry. It may be true, but it isn't literal.

There's one prophecy from Ezekiel that Ames especially wants to help Lila understand. It's a prophecy about a baby. Lila learns to write by tracing these words from Ezekiel 16 on a slate over and over again:

> As for your birth, on the day you were born your navel cord was not cut, nor were you washed with water to cleanse you, nor rubbed with salt, nor wrapped in cloths. No eye pitied you, to do any of these things for you out of compassion for you; but you were thrown out in the open field, for you were abhorred on the day you were born (Ezekiel 16:4).

But God passes by and sees this baby screaming in its own blood, with the umbilical cord still attached. And God looks down and says, "Live."

Pastor Ames calmly explains to Lila that the baby is Israel. It's figurative, he tells her, not a story about a real child. It tells us something about God and the history of Israel during the time of exile to Babylon. But Lila knows that there is more to it. "Well it's true what he says there. It's something I know about."[1]

Robinson's novel is a sort of extended exegesis of Ezekiel. At different times throughout her life, Lila has been that baby, lying in her own blood in an empty field. And at different times someone has passed by and found her and said, "Live." The Bible is unsettling because it knows Lila, and she knows it. It tells her story back to her in brutal and honest ways.

But it's not only the known, the identifiable, that catches
Lila. The incomprehensible bits sound true to her as well: the
rattling bones, the swirling chaos of Ezekiel being picked up
and set down again in an old battleground, the many-faced
creatures thrashing into thunder (Ezekiel 10). Lila thinks
about those angelic creatures with their wings and eyes and
faces. "It made as much sense as anything else. No sense at
all," Lila reflects. "If you think about a human face, it can be
something you don't want to look at . . . It can be something
you want to hide, because it pretty well shows where you've
been and what you can expect."[2]

Rowan Williams calls Lila's attraction to Ezekiel an unconventional Bible study.[3] Like Lila, encountering God in the Old
Testament takes an unconventional approach. In Ezekiel there
are too many words and images. It is a cacophony of sounds
and sights. We are lost in it, because often we are lost. The
world is sense and senseless, nature and miracle. And then
we come to discover there is a name or a word for that. We
uncover a picture and put it down with words—an image, a
story, a character that gets at something we cannot say. We
find that we are drawn into the story of God's life that is now
our story.

I expect that we make a mistake when we turn to the Bible
as an answer book. I expect that we will be disappointed if we
open its pages as if a verse here, a chapter there, will quell our
questions. Perhaps it is better to position ourselves like Lila:
here before a text swirling with God's life, words, and pictures
unfurling into our lives, passages that confuse and horrify and
baffle us—luring us farther and farther into God. We read the
Bible this way, expecting that these stories will erupt in our
lives, that they will knit our bones back together.

IN THIS BOOK I will make one modest claim, a claim issuing up from *Lila,* an affirmation not of my own making but affirmed through the history of the church: the God present in the Old Testament is the same God revealed in Jesus Christ. The character of God is uncovered in these stories, a revelation that helps Christians to recognize Jesus as God's Son. We cannot hope to understand our Christian faith without the lives, testimonies, and stories of Miriam, Esau, Job, and Naaman's enslaved child.

Ellen Davis, in her book *Getting Involved with God,* gives helpful advice that has reoriented my reading of the Old Testament. "If there is a secret to getting involved with God through the pages of Scripture," she writes, "perhaps it is this: *turn the pages slowly.*"[4] The slower we read, the more attention we give, the more we will find that the words have made a home within us.

This book is a study in slow observation. It is an extensive collection of marginalia, notes scribbled in the margins of the Bible, where the gift, terror, and hope of the Old Testament wells up in birds, children, anti-racism work, Muslim neighbors, bread, and friendship. I'm grateful for the spaces to think and read and write that made way for these observations, as many of these words were first preached to churches: Duke Memorial United Methodist Church, Chapel Hill Mennonite Fellowship, and Raleigh Mennonite Church. While these words were nurtured in libraries and study carrels and coffee shops, they were received by congregations who helped me discern where God is at work.

BUT BEFORE WE BEGIN, a few further clarifications. Throughout the book I refer to the thirty-nine books that make up the first section of the Christian Bible as the Old Testament. These books are preserved in Judaism as the Tanakh (Torah, Prophets, and Writings), or the Hebrew Bible. I've kept the language used by the church—that is, the designation of the Old Testament—because Christians believe the revelation of God is also contained in a second book called the New Testament, where God becomes enfleshed and lives among us on the earth in Jesus Christ.

In this book I do not attempt to work through the breadth of the Old Testament. One of the disciplines of my pastoral ministry is that other people tell me what to preach about, whether that is through a lectionary or a worship planning committee. Most of the chapters of this book flow from the work of preaching given to me within the various worshiping communities who have called me pastor. Others are questions presented by friends who help me wonder about something springing up in the Bible. Some are challenges from colleagues who asked me how I am troubled by the Bible and what that trouble means for how I understand God.

Finally, this isn't a book that centers our attention on the theme of violence in the Old Testament, picking out the hardest and most tragic stories of our Scriptures. Without shying away from challenging passages, I want to remind us that the Old Testament is a book of profound grace, hope, and beauty.

The Old Testament is a book of fire—a story about God's life that continues to burn away my expectations and, as a result, sets me ablaze with God's love.

1
GOD OF RECKONING

Surely, this commandment that I am commanding you today is not too hard for you, nor is it too far away. It is not in heaven, that you should say, "Who will go up to heaven for us, and get it for us so that we may hear it and observe it?" Neither is it beyond the sea, that you should say, "Who will cross to the other side of the sea for us, and get it for us so that we may hear it and observe it?" No, the word is very near to you; it is in your mouth and in your heart for you to observe.
  —DEUTERONOMY 30:11-14

Turn it, and turn it again, for everything is contained in it.
  —MISHNAH AVOT 5:22

On my way to morning prayer at St. John's Abbey in Minnesota, I take the long walk across the field, over the bridge, past the Eastern cottonwood trees, and down the walkway to the abbey church. The monks gather three times a day to pray and once for mass. During my week-long stay I've accepted the monks' gracious invitation to join them for daily prayer. On this morning, the flat face of the Bauhaus-era chapel is pink and gray against the sunrise. The bell in the tower begins to clang, summoning worshipers to gather.

I enter the side door, winding down an aisle to the dark benches reserved for community guests. This is my third summer waking early to pray with the monks. I've learned after many mornings of repetition how to sort through the row of prayer books, identifying the order for the scattered canticles and hymns. A brother monk, robed in black, comes to the aid of the confused visitors in front of me.

For a moment after one of the brothers lights the candles, the room hums with stillness. I sit with my fellow supplicants as the monks file in, genuflect to the body suspended on the cross, and take their appointed seats. One of the oldest brothers in the community sits in the closest pew, bravely and tentatively scaling the step up to his perch. A thin monk, younger than most, is the soloist this week. He leads us as we chant through the pages of psalms.

When I pray with the Benedictines, I am struck by the pauses, the long gaps the monks hold between the phrases. It's strange to my ear to hear the words drop off in the middle of the sentence. I wait with the pause, listening for the others around us to know when to start praying the words again. I remember the first summer I prayed this way, my impatience to move on, unsure of when we would know it was time to begin the words of prayer again. Now, after several weeks at St. John's, I've learned the gift in this practice of slow, communal recitation. I hear differently. The words have time to sit. There's time for them to sink down, to work their way through me.

The monks have offered me another surprising gift. Here at prayer I am held before the Scriptures, trapped with the assigned readings. Depending on the season, I find myself set before words I would not choose. Today I want nothing more than to get as far as I can from the epistle of Titus, the New Testament reading designated for this morning.

It is curious to me when Christians sense a similar distance from the Old Testament, citing the life of Jesus as a corrective for what they perceive as a fierce and wrathful God of Israel. For every passage of the Gospels where Jesus is waxing on about birds, or drawing children near in defiance of cultural respectability, there is another Jesus who assigns swaths of rich people to eternal damnation and makes unsettling judgments about what happens inside our minds. Paul's letters are chock full of frightening passages, scented with holiness and hellfire. I have seen violent readings from these epistles used to bind women to abusive marriages and to give excuse for pastors to refuse communion to whatever brand of impurity is on the market.

The Old Testament offers a different picture of God. The arc of God's story with the people of Israel is consistent—humans mess up and God is relentless in forgiveness and grace. Over and over Israel makes promises they cannot keep. Over and over again God is faithful. This narrative unfolds within the gritty details of vengeful, murderous, and at times disarmingly beautiful human lives.

BY AN UNFATHOMABLE ACT of divine grace, I have been grafted into God's fidelity to Israel. Through no merit of my own God holds on to me in the same way God held fast to a people on the brink of their self-imposed devastation. Today at morning prayer I cling to this promise in the maelstrom of my complicated relationship to the New Testament, fidgeting nervously as the monk reads from Titus. It is all I can do to keep myself from audibly announcing my frustration with the words read from the lectern: "Tell slaves to be submissive to their masters and to give satisfaction in every respect; they are not to talk back, not to pilfer, but to show complete and perfect fidelity, so that in everything they may be an ornament to the doctrine of God our Savior" (Titus 2:9-10).

These words pour down like a slow fire, and I can trace the destruction across human history. White slave masters ingrained submission into the lives of black slaves in the Americas with passages like those in Titus. The Federal Writer's Project records the stories of formerly enslaved women and men after Emancipation and several tell how the Bible, in the hands of coercive power, scaffolded the religious logic of human chattel. In one transcript, Hannah Crasson, a former enslaved woman from North Carolina, recalls how she was prohibited from reading the Bible herself, banned from learning to read at all, but that a few Bible lessons were taught to her by her masters.

Enslaved people like Hannah Crasson record how they were given 1 Timothy 6:2 ("do them service" KJV) and the reading from Titus I heard today ("do not pilfer") to consume.[1] Malinda Berry recalls that "whites unabashedly published volumes like *Selections of the Holy Bible for Negro Slaves,* but there was no Exodus story in those selections, no story of Ruth and Naomi, lest slaves encounter the linchpins whose removal from slaveholder Christianity would bring white Christianity tumbling down."[2]

White, slave-holding Christian communities understood the Bible to contain radical and dangerous notions about freedom, a subversive Old Testament narrative of a subjugated people who fled captivity in Egypt and were led by God into a promised land. They were right to be fearful of the blueprint of freedom set down in the Old Testament. Over time a Moses rose up among them, in the form of a petite woman who had escaped from slavery to the north and suffered from injury-induced epilepsy. Her name was Araminta Ross, known to many as Harriet Tubman. Once, when a man was asked if the slaves she brought to freedom were afraid along the way, he answered no, because the "Lord has given Moses power."[3]

Slaveholders—and their ministers—had to suppress the Old Testament narrative of freedom in order for slavery to flourish in the Americas. They did their best to keep stories of freedom from the minds of Harriet Tubman and those who followed her out of slavery. Handpicked passages from the New Testament, combined with fidelity to the Word of God, did the job.

When we read Titus during morning prayer, I can imagine the lines of wooden benches before a white priest much like the one before me today, reciting these words over rows of black faces. Submission. Fidelity. Dogma. Holiness. All intertwined into a catastrophic misconstrual of the Bible for the sake of turning human bodies into capitalist profit.

I stand before these words, receive them back, and dare not look away. This reading binds me to a past that is never past. With the monks, standing before this reading from Titus, I've come to see that the Bible is a reckoning, where we come face to face with what we have done with the Bible or what the Bible has done to us. We cannot escape the interpretive communities we form, and these communities matter for how we will read the Bible today. Whenever we read the Bible, we participate in a history. In that history are those who have turned the good news into both joy and terror.

Indebtedness—this is a discipline I have learned here at prayer among the monks. The Benedictines take time each morning to remember those in their community who have died. Today at morning prayer we pause in memory of Brother Alfred who died in 1866, and Brother John who left this world in 1991. The lives that came before us linger, whether we name them or not. We are indebted to interpretive communities that have formed us to latch on to certain words, ideas, and passages. Other stories we are taught to ignore or repress. Every time we read the Bible we bring with us the generations before us, what they pass down—all of it is within us.

I am grateful for communities and practices that pry me into confrontation with these discomfiting passages like the words of submission from Titus. I'm grateful that the monks do not shy away from them or hide the difficult parts from me. Without the text this morning, I would miss the occasion for my own reckoning. Titus reminds me of my own willingness to coexist alongside modern-day slavery, even as this epistle remembers a Christian tradition that abetted the enslavement of African people. More often than I care to think, I thought-lessly shuttle a wedge of Brie cheese from Whole Foods into my cart, a product made cheaply by the labor of incarcerated bodies, people who work without pay. I live undisturbed alongside human beings trafficked for labor in nail salons and restaurants. I have assumed that prison sentences and bail bonds keep me and my people safe. I can go weeks without thinking of asylum-seeking immigrants placed in holding cells at the border for indefinite periods of time. *See what horrors we justified, what you justify today*, I hear in the echoing space after the epistle is read.

THIS MORNING IN THE ABBEY we hear another word, this time a word of judgment. A gentle monk—bent by age, a ring of hair around his bald pate—utters lines from the book of Judith, in the Apocrypha:

> Woe to the nations that rise up against my people!
> The Lord Almighty will take vengeance on them in the
> day of judgment;
> he will send fire and worms into their flesh;
> they shall weep in pain for ever.

It's incongruous, the words and the frail body of the monk who says them. We are saying words we do not understand, words on which I cannot get a purchase on this morning full with light and song.

But these words were not written for me on this day. They are words for the enslaved, words of protest, words of judgment that well up from lives terrorized by sexualized violence, torture, kidnapping, and slavery. They are words that express God's fierce solidarity with the marginalized. This is a record of imprecatory prayers rising up from a Japanese internment camp, from a Hopi mission boarding school, from an eviction court. They are words that hold space for those in the presence of terror and hopelessness, a reminder that God burns like fire for them. I suspect that these words are preserved for all of us, should we find that one day we need them, too. And if that time should come, we have a community that has gone before us, that shows us the way of fierce survival.

In this way, reading Scripture is an invitation to being undone—a way to a God who invites us into the world of another. Rowan Williams writes that God makes a way to us in a peculiar way through the Bible—"by telling a certain kind of story from a human point of view."[4] These stories told from human perspective carry us toward God, never forcing us there but revealing a God who patiently and slowly helps us work through our images of God and our conceptions of divine anger. We are invited to witness the lives of people in Scripture who struggled with God's presence and God's absence.

In my tradition, the Mennonite church, I think of this way of reading the Bible as the spiritual practice of *Gelassenheit*, or self-surrender. As I receive the words from the monks, words that fall like stones, I remember that *Gelassenheit* returns me to the root *lassen*—"to let or allow." God lets this story stay here as we make our way through the devastation of history, praying that we will be called to account for our part.

ON ANOTHER MORNING I walk to the abbey for prayer, my steps heavy with rainwater. My attempts at dodging the flooded lowlands are largely unsuccessful, and now my shoes squeak with embarrassing sharpness against the stone floors of the silent abbey church. Today we chant the words of Jeremiah 31:12:

> They will come and shout for joy on Mount Zion;
> They will stream to the blessing of the Lord,
> To the corn, the new wine and the oil,
> To the lamb and the cattle.
> Their life will be like a watered garden.
> They will never be weary again.

Everyone I talk to is glad for the rains. "We've needed this," a brother tells me, as we strike up a conversation in line for breakfast waffles. "He covers the heaven with clouds," we prayed in unison earlier that hour. "He prepares the rain for the earth, making mountains sprout with grass and with plants to serve our needs" (Psalm 146:10).

We say these words, too, remembering that within us—within those who are bound together to read and pray—are Scriptures that wrap themselves around our world and draw it close. This is another seeing, another surprise.

I had to learn to see like this. And it was the rabbis who first taught me how to read with the Bible.

I came to the rabbis by chance when I was still a teenager, placed in an undergraduate Old Testament course with a professor who finished her education at a rabbinical college. Though a Christian, she taught me the Bible through these masterful teachers whom she turned to as our guides for grappling with the Old Testament. Over time, the rabbis became my companions. The rabbis showed me skilled and often playful interpretations of the Bible. Decades later, I cannot read the Bible without seeing in my mind an image of the rabbis Hillel and Shammai hunched over their manuscripts, arguing over the significance of the Hebrew letter *alef* or debating the ethics of the *Akedah,* the story in Genesis of the binding of Isaac.

Later, I learned that these teachers, the rabbis, were equally complicated reading partners. It's a path of disillusionment I suppose all students must travel with beloved teachers. In his writings, the rabbinic scholar Daniel Boyarin has taught me to notice that the rabbis were ambivalent in their assessment of women's lives and roles, male scholars who were products of an androcentric culture.[5] Another reckoning, I suppose.

But my imagination is shaped by the early rabbinic exegetical practice of grappling and dialogue, unfettered by divisions of body and soul. I continue to return to the rabbis as friends who show me how to play, weep, and nurse the wounds inflicted by the Bible's words. They taught me to love the words themselves, every *alef* and *tav*, to turn them and turn them again.

THERE'S ONE STORY from the rabbis that reoriented me to the authority of communal readings of Scripture after a lifetime of being trained in individualistic hermeneutics. In this story the rabbis are arguing over the status of a clay oven, an attention to the minutia of life that I relish.

Argumentation is a consistent act in the drama of rabbinic interpretation. A robust debate is par for the course of figuring out the Bible, a wrestling that reminds us of the seriousness and the intricacy of Scripture. It was worthy of raised voices and the occasional pounded fist.

In this story the rabbis wonder if a particular type of oven is ritually clean or unclean. Rabbi Eliezer, considered the most learned sage of his generation, stands alone against the interpretation given by the community. The oven—he tells them definitively, with clear and unwavering confidence—is clean. His companions will not back down, so Eliezer calls upon creation to confirm his judgment. If he is right, he tells the other rabbis, the carob tree before him will move. In response, the tree, pulling itself up by the roots, moves down the lane.

Yet the sages are unchanged in their judgment. A carob tree, they say, cannot be used as a source of proof. Growing more frustrated, Eliezer declares, "If I am right, and the oven is clean, let this stream before me flow backward." Immediately, the current reverses course.

Still, the rabbis in the majority are unmoved. Distraught, Eliezer declares, "If I am right, let the walls of the House of Study bend inward." Yet, even as the walls bend, the sages refuse to change their collective ruling.

Finally, Eliezer calls upon God to weigh in on the matter of the clay oven. A voice from heaven declares that Eliezer is correct: the oven is clean. But even now the rabbis stand by their original ruling, the decision of the majority. Rabbi Joshua responds to the divine voice by quoting a passage from Deuteronomy: "It is not in heaven."

Assuming those of us reading this story are perplexed by the audacity to rebuke God using the Torah, Rabbi Jeremiah goes on to explain what Joshua means. The Torah is no longer in heaven. "Since the Torah has been given already on Mount Sinai, we do not pay attention to a heavenly voice, for You have written in Your Torah, 'Decide according to the majority.'" The heavenly voice responds in laughter, saying, "My children have defeated me!"

Rabbi Jeremiah's words back to the heavenly voice contain a sliver of Deuteronomy 30:

> Surely, this commandment that I am commanding you today is not too hard for you, nor is it too far away. It is not in heaven, that you should say, 'Who will go up to heaven for us, and get it for us so that we may hear it and observe it?' Neither is it beyond the sea, that you should say, 'Who will cross to the other side of the sea for us, and get it for us so that we may hear it and observe it?'

"No, the word is very near to you," the passage from Deuteronomy continues, "it is in your mouth and in your heart for you to observe" (Deuteronomy 30:14). When the rabbis read these words from the Torah, they understand that a transmission takes place as God's Word moves from heaven to earth, into the care and keeping of God's people. Once it goes out to the people, God releases God's own claim on the work of proclamation, interpretation, and application. Scripture becomes the work of the people, our task to discover.

The story of Eliezer and the clay oven, like many of the interpretive traditions of Judaism in the first centuries CE, is marked by surprise. Along the way readers encounter and uncover, noticing the elaborate details of the Scriptures. The rabbis pay attention to a change in a verb, a missing pronoun. They mark a character mysteriously absent from the story and words with similar roots: these become ingrained meanings, spaces, and silences. From this fertile plot, morals and exegesis blossom.

Embedded in the story of the clay oven is a conviction that Scripture's interpretation belongs to the communities that read it. The words formed on the page can mean nothing unless they are taken and read. Each generation discovers something new there. The people of God in each age must encounter the Bible again with new questions that come to life with our histories in tow.

A posture of vulnerability—toward both the Bible and the communities that form around it—is a disarming position to take, and it has been this way throughout the history of the church. In the third century, the African theologian Augustine of Hippo responded to complaints from Christian learners who were frustrated by the opacity of the Bible. In irritation they protested to their pastor, wondering why God didn't send angels to explain to them what they read in the Scriptures. That, Augustine explained in *De doctrina christiana,* would be missing the point. The work of interpretation is not for instruction alone; it is for creating a temple out of God's people, a task that leads us toward love, "pouring soul into soul."[6]

Augustine reminds me that the faith questions we carry around in our pockets have remained fairly constant over a couple thousand years. Generations of Bible-readers scratch their heads, also looking for answers. But Augustine offers us the same response he did to those Bible readers in his day. We do not wait for angels. We sit and we talk. Augustine tells us this is love itself—to discover the Bible with one another.

A FEW YEARS AGO I was at an ecumenical conference where each morning we sat at large, round tables and introduced ourselves to the other participants. One morning I sat next to a woman who asked to hear more about the Mennonites. She was especially interested, for reasons I still cannot figure out, in our preaching, and in particular the length of my sermons. I explained that my part of the sermon was no longer than a quarter hour. She was taken aback. "Our pastor preaches 30 to 45 minutes each week!" she exclaimed. "He could never get away with a sermon that short!"

I told her that our preaching, in total, lasted about that long as well. I told her about sharing time. I explained that each Sunday we have a time in our service when we respond to God's Word preached among us. In our Mennonite church, the interpretation of the Bible doesn't belong to the preacher alone. It belongs to us, to God's people. We ask questions, comment on what we've heard, fill in the gaps, tell each other "thank you" for the work done here among us.

Each Sunday the preaching begins in the pulpit. But that's never where it ends. Each Sunday preaching extends to the community, the other priests in this church. Each Sunday we're given the opportunity to wonder aloud: *Did you receive*

the good news? *And if not, what work do we still have to do?*
How does the good news become real here, at this time?

It's not a time for people to argue with the pastor, or to
blast one another on doctrine or hermeneutics, or to comment
on the questionable quality of the preacher's humor. Those
things happen from time to time, but that's not why we open
this space. Instead, this is the time when we as Christ's body
do the work of discerning if and how the good news has been
proclaimed in and among us through our singing, praying,
reading Scripture, and preaching.

Sharing in this way is a long-rooted tradition in Ana-
baptism, a practice called *zeugnis* in German, translated as
"testimony." We don't know much about these moments of
communal discernment, mentioned only in passing by perse-
cuted 16th century Anabaptists on the run, but we do know
why they happened. Our Anabaptist forebears read in the
Bible that every person is gifted, that each one of us is a priest.
We need others to confirm God's Word, and to help us think
through what has been said. We trust that God is coming to a
decision through us.

Lydia Harder reminds us that in the free church, "Not the
state, not specialized theologians, nor hierarchical authorities
were to be the final judge of the Bible's meaning."[7] For me, this
is the strangest, most provocative practice that I've discovered
in the Mennonite churches where I have worshiped. We believe
that our communal decision-making has authority, that our
decisions stick in heaven and on earth (Matthew 18:18). The
Word is not in heaven. It is very near, indeed.

EACH YEAR on Good Friday I join others in my church to
push chairs together, forming a semi-circle in the room where

we meet for worship. The light fades as evening grows to night. We read to one another the story of Jesus' final hours of earthly life. It's the story we tell on this night every year, dimming the lights and dissolving our meeting place into darkness.

This year I asked Jeff to take up one of the readings. At random I assigned him the second passage from Mark's gospel, in which Jesus and his followers go to Gethsemane to pray. The disciples can't stay awake. "Simon, are you asleep? Could you not keep awake one hour?" Jesus says. "Keep awake and pray that you may not come into the time of trial; the spirit indeed is willing, but the flesh is weak" (Mark 14:37-38).

A decade ago, while only in mid-life, Jeff suffered a stroke. He carries the marks of that brain injury in his gait and right arm. He and I talk about the work of his recovery and the many years in which he taught and re-taught his brain to eat, dress, move, think, and read.

On this night, Jeff makes his way to the pulpit, holding his little Bible with his working hand. He begins to read, slowly and deliberately. Each word is like a pebble dropped in the sea. *He. Came. And. Found. Them. Sleeping.* The words fall, one by one. Later someone will tell me that to hear Jeff is like watching seeds being planted. A patient labor.

From that night on, I hear Jeff's voice whenever I read in Mark about Jesus praying to his Father. Jesus is crippled by worry, grief, and fear. His words fall slowly and deliberately onto the ground, a watering of tears. They fall one by one, received into the waiting ground. "Their life will be like a watered garden," I hear Jeremiah 31:12 whisper from the pages.

When Jeff reads Scripture, we are re-formed to hear this passage in new ways. Our imaginations change us and change the Bible before us. The bodies that read, the bodies that speak the words, matter for us. It matters which bodies spoke those words in the past, who reads them today, in what communities, and to whom they are spoken. All of it is a reckoning, letting the words work among us.

We come to the Bible carrying the past with us. Mingled with the words on the page are the interpretations and stories, communities and traumas, histories and experiences we bear in our bodies. "First you believe and then you see," I remember hearing. To come to the Old Testament in hope and love, we first name what we believe, discover all that we carry with us, lay it bare, and then begin again.

2

God of Neighbors

You shall keep my statutes. You shall not let your animals breed with a different kind; you shall not sow your field with two kinds of seed; nor shall you put on a garment made of two different materials.
　—LEVITICUS 19:19

To have an outside, to listen to what comes from outside—oh miracle of exteriority!
　—EMMANUEL LEVINAS, *DIFFICULT FREEDOM*

On Valentine's Day, a note arrived, shoved into the mail slot of my neighbor's door. Pulling out the crisp flyer, she discovered two interlaced hearts in swirling font that proclaimed "Love your own race!" and "Stop homosexuality and race mixing!"

The notes are part of a recruiting mission by members of a local Ku Klux Klan chapter. In the bottom corner, written with the same saccharine lettering, are the words "God's Laws, Don't Forget!"

Campaigns like these—hate flyers carefully placed in plastic bags to protect their contents from the wind and the rain—happen on occasion here in North Carolina. The white supremacists who leave these warnings around our neighborhood make their case through the distortion of biblical commandments like those found in the book of Leviticus. Anti-miscegenation is read back into these directives because the Holiness Code, they imagine, is invested in separation and purity. "You shall not let your animals breed with a different kind; you shall not sow your field with two kinds of seed; nor shall you put on a garment made of two different materials," says Leviticus 19:19.

Throughout the eighteenth and nineteenth centuries, white supremacists exploited biblical passages about separation to advance ideologies of racial distinction. Racism was mingled with pseudoscience, fueled by fears of black men threatening the future dominance of white men in the United States. There was particular anxiety about white women in sexual relationships with black men, the ultimate spurning of white patriarchal power.

Hate notes littering neighborhoods in my city are a reminder that some read biblical laws as on-going demands for separation. These become fodder for dogmas of anxiety in which distinction from neighbors is considered holy work. For a long time it was difficult for me to read Leviticus, impossible to place myself in a world set to maintain purity. Each day I try to cultivate a life of understanding and respect among my neighbors, a world rich in what we have in common and in our uniqueness. While I've often shrugged my way through Leviticus, it could be that there's something here for me after all.

TO UNDERSTAND what God intends for us in the Holiness Code, forms of life put down in books like Leviticus, we begin with the story of God's people as they receive the words of the Law. We return to Israel's life in the desert.

The words of Leviticus are caked in sand. They are words read in the aching heat of midday. In the Old Testament we learn that the words of Leviticus are read between meals of manna as monotonous days stretch into weeks and years. I wandered this stretch of the wilderness years ago. In the summers I spent in Palestine and Israel, friends and I would take our weekends away from our archaeological dig to trudge through the shallow *wadis* and around twisted slate rock formations. In the midday, the sun severe and high, we would shelter and sleep until it was safe to move on.

I can feel that dry heat blistering the words of Leviticus. They are written for a desert people who know want and survival, a people on the run. They are words that prepare them for a life they do not yet possess, a way of life that is yet to be. The Hebrews have escaped from slavery in Egypt, led by Miriam, Aaron, and Moses, and into the wilderness. There they receive the commandments for the Promised Land, the terrain of a new life still on the horizon. The people are now captives to the desert and to wandering for forty years. They are a generation waiting for their wayward parents to die away.

But God is getting them ready, preparing them for a new life. Those who pick up these words were born into this wandering. Their only food has been a gift so strange they called it *manna*—a word translated "What is it?"—it evoked such surprise and confusion in its recipients. At night a divine gift—quail—floats across the land. But there is another life waiting for them, and here in the wilderness God gives the people the instructions for the world opening before them.

God gets invested in the ordinary stuff of eating and sleeping, bathing and worshiping. Wilda Gafney writes that "Leviticus concerns itself with everything your body squeezes or squirts out, extrudes, expels, leaks, or flakes, with the exception of snot, spittle, urine, feces, and vomit."[1] Unlike the ancient Israelites, on Sunday morning my church does not spend our time considering what to do with a crushed limb, the specifics around rescuing animals on the Sabbath, or the rules for weaving together different textiles. Few of us have puzzled over whether we should eat bats, and we avoid graphic descriptions of nocturnal emissions, oozing sores, and menstrual blood.

For similar reasons, throughout much of church history Christians considered the book of Leviticus irrelevant for the lives of those who follow Jesus. When early missionaries translated the Bible, they often left Leviticus out altogether, erasing it from the canon.[2]

Leviticus can come across as an oddity, a list of old and nonsensical rituals. The challenge for contemporary readers is to scrutinize the world of Leviticus for the places where social norms are dictated by healthy, Israelite males, where punishments are meted out unequally, and where slavery is normalized. Leviticus invites us into a discipline for being disturbed by the right things.

When Leviticus makes a rare appearance in our pulpits or lectionaries, it is because an express link to the New Testament emerges. For this reason Leviticus 19 is preserved in the Revised Common Lectionary: "You shall not take vengeance or bear a grudge against any of your people, but you shall love your neighbor as yourself" (19:18). We know these words. They are said by Jesus, echoed back in the gospel of Mark (12:30-31). And here we should pause. Even if the church does not spend significant time with Leviticus, Jesus—God in flesh—treasured these teachings with enough care to quote them to his followers.

The details of Leviticus—lived out in the bodies of God's people, in the daily reminders of food, children, water, and wounds—remain here for us to discover. These include first instructions about the tabernacle, a tent where God's spirit is present among God's people. From here the teachings spread out. Not only will they make a tabernacle with cloth and wood, the people will construct a tabernacle with their lives. The cornerstone of this tabernacle will be justice. The teachings will distinguish God's people from both those in the land they have left and those in the land to which they will go.

For ancient Israel, holiness takes on spatial character. Unlike the peoples around them, both the Egyptians of the past and Canaanites of their future, the Hebrew people have God as the only source of holiness. People, objects, rituals—none of these has power on its own, no created thing possesses the power to harm or heal. Care for Israel has one source, and that source is God. There is no need to lift up or cower before powerful leaders or stone objects, no need to worry over the luckiness of beard length or the possibility that a birthmark signifies looming death. God is the sole nurturer, protector, and savior of Israel.

It was the Jewish biblical scholar Jacob Milgrom whose writings helped me learn to explore Leviticus as a set of ritual symbols that tell us something about God's protection and care for God's people. One of Milgrom's insights came from his study of the Levitical restriction against eating any four-legged animal that does not chew its cud or have a split hoof. It was no coincidence, noted Milgrom, that the approved animals, limited in their geographic context to sheep, goats, and cows, were the same three animals that were sanctioned for sacrificial offering. In other words, these animals are "eligible for the human table because they are eligible for God's altar/table."[3]

Milgrom goes on to explain that "the dining table symbolically becomes an altar, and all the diners are symbolically priests." In the ritual we discover that "all of life is sacred and inviolable."[4] If we are careful excavators in Leviticus's ground, we discover the richness of this book.

IT TAKES WORK to notice these connections. And even among chapters and verses that appear to be useful for the Christian community—rules that make sense to us, rules that tell us to pay fair wages, not to steal, and give to the poor—even here commandments strange to us slip in. The assigned passage from the Revised Common Lectionary for Leviticus 19 does some careful gerrymandering to step around these verses: "When you offer a sacrifice of well-being to the Lord, offer it in such a way that it is acceptable on your behalf. It shall be eaten on the same day you offer it, or on the next day; and anything left over until the third day shall be consumed in fire" (Leviticus 19:5-6). The reading ends before we encounter a verse that says, "You shall not let your animals breed with a different kind. You shall not sow your field with two kinds of seed; nor shall you put on a garment made of two different materials" (Leviticus 19:19).

But these verses also matter. Leviticus teaches us that holiness is more than keeping yourself uncontaminated. Instead, purity is a ritual that embeds justice in the body. The ritual laws in Leviticus stitch together a form of life for a people, or as Wilda Gafney writes, it is a "text about how to live in relationship: how to live in relationship to God and how to live in relation to others in the community."[5] Purity for Israel was a constant reminder that every part of life was significant to God, a reminder that God gets into everything.

The Torah, the first five books of the Bible, provides the form of life to move into the Promised Land—a new place with new neighbors. The Hebrew writers structured their writing to put the most important teachings at the center. Here at the midpoint of the Torah is where we find Leviticus. And at the very center, forming the crease, the place where the pages fall open, is Leviticus 19. This chapter is the cornerstone—holiness inseparable from justice. In this chapter, Leviticus repeats the same words over and over again, more times than anywhere else in the Torah: "I am the Lord." Mary Douglas says these words—"I am the Lord"—are like precious jewels, scattered around the pages of the chapter.[6] They are decorations that cause you to catch your breath when you encounter them, words you want to hold up to the light.

The laws, the rules, the regulations: all of this is about getting into God's life, getting the body inside of "I am the Lord." Douglas reminds us that ancient people passed down their way of life through rituals, their most treasured cultural gifts held within communal actions and practices. Douglas points us to the chapters before and after Leviticus 19, drawing our attention to the fact that what people do for God is paralleled by how Israel will treat her neighbors. We discover "I am the Lord" in the bodies of the people.

Leviticus is a book about getting a people inside of God's life, and then making a world that looks like God's justice.

What the Hebrews knew in Egypt—what they will encounter again in Canaan—are gods of stone and steel, gods set up to exact punishment and reward, gods both cruel and capricious. Worst of all, these gods are powerless slabs of rock and metal.

Adonai—the God who sets captives free, who feeds in the wilderness, who brings the Hebrews to the other side of the Jordan, who brings life—this is the God the people are called to follow, acting out a way of life through their bodies. The commandment points the way toward a life like God's life in time and space.

In one sense we recognize the absence of God's justice in some parts of Leviticus. From our vantage point thousands of years later we bear witness to a people who escaped slavery only to enslave others. We grapple with sexual purity demanded of women but not of men. We see physical punishment enacted with little attention to power. And here, within this truth, Leviticus helps us to see how the current of God's life persists even in the face of human failure. In Leviticus there is always enough, the edges of the field full for those who are in need. In God's life the elderly and the sick are honored and celebrated. In God's life people who are deaf and physically atypical are treated with dignity.

Martin Buber writes that the command to love one's neighbor ends with this pronouncement—"I am the Lord"—because God is telling those of us who read it how to interpret the previous words, a command to love our neighbor. Buber writes that the Hasidic rabbis heard God saying, "You think that I am far away from you, but in your love for your neighbor you will find Me; not in his love for you but in your love for him."[7]

We're indefinitely in the process of figuring out what God's life looks like here and now, how to take these words passed down to us and to work them out in the grain of our lives. What are the idols? Who are the enemies? Where do we see the cornerstone of justice? How does our life echo back those words: "I am the Lord"? What are our failures? How can we scrutinize and talk back to the "common sense" institutions and assumptions of holiness that dictate our social and religious world? Who stands at the margins of dominant power and can lead us in the work of recognizing God's holiness?

These questions remind us that we are not so different from those ancient people in the desert. We, too, are pulled into superstition, drawn into belief in a bleak world out for our destruction. We, too, set our days to the rhythm of scarcity, working endlessly and without rest. We, too, have believed the lie that only one people, one family, one tribe can win. The work given to us is to see our neighbor's dignity reflecting back in our own, and in doing so to see that God was there all along.

IMAM MOHAMED ABU-TALEB meets me in the parking lot, the wind whipping his white robe around his ankles. We walk together through the sprawling campus of the Islamic Association. Thousands come to the building's *masjid* to pray every week. The building is also home to an Islamic school, and I can hear the sounds of children laughing and playing soccer as we walk by an open window.

In every room I pass by I see a poster of three silhouetted faces. In 2015, Deah Barakat, Yusor Abu-Salha, and Yusor's sister, Razan, were murdered outside their apartment complex in Chapel Hill, thirty miles from where Mohamed and I stand. Their murder was a hate crime, a vicious act of xenophobic cruelty by a white neighbor. The three young people were graduates of Imam Mohamed's school and belonged to the community of the Islamic Center.

Deah and Yusor were training to be dentists. They spent their school breaks providing dental care in countries where children do not have access to these medical services. I remember looking at their faces in the newspaper. They were so young. "Our Three Winners," the words below the posters at the Islamic Center read. Over the years, Mohamed has watched anti-Muslim hate and rhetoric surge through our country.

Mohamed and I talk as we move to the kitchen. We take tabbouleh and hummus on our trays, along with spiced eggplant. We sit in the wide empty space of the cafeteria while he tells me about his family and this community. He's been here for a year, not much longer than me. We both have three-year-olds. We discuss the impending birth of his second child, the pastoral care needs of the people in his care, and the current political climate in North Carolina.

In the fall a few people from our church visit the Islamic Association. The Muslim community invites groups like our congregation to join them for evening prayer at the *masjid* and to learn about Islam. Their reaction to the increasing violence and hatred toward those who practice Islam is to open their doors wider, to educate, and to sustain friendships across religious lines.

And so it is that a group of Mennonites gather outside the center as the sun is setting. We take off our shoes and put them on a rack beside the long rows of green carpet. We slip in as prayer begins, planting our bodies behind a group of women with their foreheads pressed gently to the ground. Their little ones circle around, coming in and out of the room, joining in prayer before popping up again to somersault or cuddle with their mothers. We stand as the community finishes. As the women before us get up from prayer, they are surprised to see us, surprise followed by delight.

A woman comes toward me. Her name is Hajalah, she says, as she shakes my hand. "I am so glad you have come," she tells me, her voice bubbling up through her *hijab*. "Sometimes we feel so alone. We are so afraid. And then visitors come and we know we are not alone. It means so much to me. Thank you for coming. Thank you. Thank you." I can see through the slit in her flowered *hijab* that her eyes are filled with tears. She hugs me, holding me to her for a long time, then takes my hands again. "Thank you." All the fear and loneliness, and suddenly someone is there. We are filled with light.

The day after Donald Trump is elected president of the United States, the first email I send is to Mohamed. When we met, he told me that most people think incidents of violence toward Muslims spike after terrorist attacks. It's not true. Most acts of hatred toward Muslims happen during elections. The violence peaks as the rhetoric of otherness, fueled by a desire for purity, pulls us away from one another.

On the news that evening I see the picture of a woman whose *hijab* was ripped from her head at the grocery store. I hear of white adults spitting anti-Muslim slurs at children, Latinos being told that "their time is up," white children in elementary schools chanting, "Build a wall."

I'll write to Mohamed throughout the year. An anti-Muslim group is gathering at the state capitol building. This rumor, that rumor. How can we be there for you? What do you need? What could we possibly do?

In the background of this interreligious solidarity—of showing up for our Muslim neighbors—I am brought back to the nagging anxieties of the KKK flyers that appeared in my neighbor's mailbox. *God's Laws, Don't Forget.* And yet, even here Leviticus may surprise us. We find that mixing together, whether it was cattle or seed or textiles, is not anathema in itself. Instead, mixtures are the stuff of holiness. Rather than a violation of an imagined divinely appointed order—as members of the KKK have assumed—mixed things are the holiest, set aside for holy use, made special by being under the auspices of the priests. Interwoven materials and combined metals illuminate the tabernacle and the priestly garments (Exodus 27:1-19, 28:6-8).

Jacob Milgrom reminds us that the exception to intermixing for ordinary Israelites was the inclusion of a single thread of blue woven into the wool tassels worn by every adult male. In the book of Numbers we hear that every time Israelites see this blue cord, they are reminded of the call to holiness, the holiness of the tabernacle extending into the life of everyday people.[8]

Throughout Leviticus there are other reminders to the people that the spatial form of God's holiness calls them deeper into relationship with the people who are their neighbors. It is in this book of the Torah where we read that the people of God are to treat those who are foreign-born as if they were native-born. "Love them as yourself, for you were foreigners in Egypt," Leviticus 19:34 (NIV) reminds them. In the same chapter the people are told to keep the edges of the harvest for the "poor and the foreigner" (19:10 NIV).

But if we are looking for the strongest remembrance of the absence of any divinely ordered prohibition against mixing among the people in the land, it is the lack of any legislation against intermarriage. Considering the number of types of marriage between Israelites that are outlawed in Leviticus, it's a striking omission. Whatever spatial forms of holiness are maintained by the people through their daily actions, marriage would not disrupt their call to be different from the nations around them. Even when the Old Testament does require separation from other tribes, these warnings stand in tension with marriages like that of the Moabite Ruth, who carries on the line of King David through marriage to the Israelite, Boaz.

AT THE CENTER of holiness, at the center of Leviticus, is justice built into the bodies of the people, the land, the community. God's life emanates from this center.

Those who propagate anti-miscegenation laws, those who threaten our Muslim neighbors—they are warned in Leviticus. As it is today, so it was then. The people who get hold of the teachings of the law begin to distort them. They use these teachings to swindle and cheat. The oppressed become the oppressors. God's people break God's law. They turn their separateness into boundaries that damage and disfigure.

I recognize this tendency—this desire to stay clear of religious trouble—in my own church tradition. For Mennonites, nonconformity is both a source of pain and hope. It provides a theological foundation to stand against participation in militarized violence. The long line of faithfulness to the gospel of peace is rooted here. At other times, nonconformity in the hands of white Mennonites imperiled the witness of the gospel. Throughout the period of the civil rights movement in the 1960s, Mennonites were at odds as to the form our political engagement should take. Should Mennonite separation from the world—our Romans 12 call to "not be conformed to this world"—take the form of removing ourselves from the political movement for black freedom?

Vincent Harding, alongside other Mennonites of color, demonstrated that the tradition of nonconformity could be envisioned as a call to oppose racial segregation in bathrooms, buses, courtrooms, and classrooms. Harding told Mennonites that the "race war" was simply another form of violent worldly incursion against which Anabaptists must distinguish ourselves. He utilized the language of nonconformity, peacemaking, and love to call Mennonites to this new theological challenge.[9]

Harding wrote that, ironically, the response from white Mennonites was "non-conformity to the ways of this world [while they] slavishly and silently conformed to the American attitudes of race and segregation."[10] The Mennonite historian Felipe Hinojosa explains, "White Mennonites did not so much disagree with black civil rights leaders as they feared what civil rights engagement might actually mean for them. White Mennonites questioned whether they were suited for political protest on the streets or promoting legislative action."[11]

WHEN WE READ Leviticus 19, we find familiar words. We hear commandments about the form justice will take as the people of God move out of the desert and into a new land. We hear a modified form of the Ten Commandments given to Moses on Mt Sinai.

Here, on the fringe of the desert, these commandments put flesh on the bone, muscle and sinew giving God's life shape and movement. These words become ritualized in the community. Leviticus shows us how God's law is dynamic, taking on new forms, facing the new challenges of the time and place in which God's people will live. God's life works itself out within different people in every age, life springing up within us.

In each generation we find ourselves standing on the crest of a new promised land, a world brimming with potential if we are willing to see it. A world without prisons, a world without hunger, a land just out of reach. And we are stretching out, learning the way there, learning what we must resist in this place—the temptations here in this land that assimilate us into injustice, that pattern our lives according to the accepted forms of oppression. We stand here looking out and telling each other to be wary. As it has always been, we show each other the way, rereading the words of our wilderness people, passed down through the generations—words full of promise, pointing us back to our neighbors.

3
GOD OF VICTIMS

Then the LORD *rained on Sodom and Gomorrah sulfur and fire from the* LORD *out of heaven; and he overthrew those cities, and all the Plain, and all the inhabitants of the cities, and what grew on the ground. But Lot's wife, behind him, looked back, and she became a pillar of salt.*

Abraham went early in the morning to the place where he had stood before the LORD*; and he looked down toward Sodom and Gomorrah and toward all the land of the Plain, and saw the smoke of the land going up like the smoke of a furnace.*

—GENESIS 19:24-28

How could I imagine Parchman would pull me to it and refuse to let go? And how could I conceive that Parchman was past, present, and future all at once?

—JESAMYN WARD, *SING, UNBURIED, SING*

At times the Old Testament prepares ground for neighborliness to flourish. At other times we are gripped by the realities of the destructive forces deeply buried in us, pervasive evil that rips apart human communities.

Genesis 19 holds one of these latter stories. The destruction of the city of Sodom described in this chapter is a shocking act of violence, both in its context and in this story's many uses as a weapon of exclusion. In the church in which I was raised, the story of Sodom and Gomorrah's untimely end was used to justify the marginalization of LGBTQ people; thus my own anxieties are palpable as I read this story. I suspect many of us sense a heavy burden each time we come across this text, or have had it hurled at us in debates over human sexuality.

And yet, I've been returned to this story as I've seen its resonance—not in the exclusion of LGBTQ people but as I've grappled with persistence of systemic violence and my witting and unwitting participation in these systems. Genesis 18–19 is a case study in oppressive systems, a narrative that invites us to consider a violence so pervasive, so destructive for the people who are caught up in it, that it takes a miraculous and devastating intervention from God to undo it. In this way, I've found that the story of Sodom and Gomorrah reorients my notions of justice and compassion. It's a story that draws me into a longing for both God's fiery justice and God's miraculous redemption.

Because of my pacifist convictions, it is not easy for me to admit how much I need Genesis 19. When the world is a chaos of terror, I long for a God who is able to destroy the cities of Sodom and Gomorrah, a God who restores the world by rejecting the evil we've routinized in our daily lives, the injustice we've enshrined in the structures that organize our society, the oppression we've normalized in our culture. I need a God who hears the cries of children trafficked in back alleys, who sees those who do not know how to escape intimate partner violence, who reaches down for people whose brothers and fathers are lost to the prison system. I want a God who becomes flame, ignited by their misery, blazing with their pain, engulfing the systems of power that victimize them, turning all of it to ash. Redemption by fire.

In Genesis 19, I discover a God who is with and for the most vulnerable of our world. God hears these voices and asks us to hear them, too—to let that compassion burn in our hearts and to long for the restoration of the victims, the empowerment of the disempowered.

WE ARE INTRODUCED to the city of Sodom in Genesis 18 as we overhear a conversation between God and Abraham. In the background of this dialogue is Lot, the nephew of Abraham, who has settled with his family in nearby Sodom. After some internal questioning, God reluctantly divulges to Abraham the plans God has made for the looming destruction of Lot's chosen home.

The city will face its demise because of something God hears. Something is amiss in Sodom. On my harder days, when I am convinced that my prayer is spoken into the void of my own conscience, I remember God's words in Genesis: "How great is the outcry against Sodom and Gomorrah and how very grave their sin! I must go down and see whether they have done altogether according to the outcry that has come to me; and if not, I will know" (Genesis 18:20).

How great is the outcry. We pause here to listen to the inhabitants of the city who are desperate for liberation, for salvation. We imagine the terror of life in that community. In Genesis we can glean that predatory sex is daily fare for the vulnerable people of Sodom.

So deep is the abuse that, when a crowd of men come to prey upon the visitors lodged at his house for the night, Lot willingly offers up his own daughters to be raped.

Lot offers up his children to sexualized violence without a second thought, their lives an acceptable exchange to the men who snarl outside his door.

How great is the outcry. And in response, sulfur and ash rain on Sodom and Gomorrah. When I read this story, I can imagine that it is Lot's daughters whom God hears—victims of abuse at the hands of violent citizens, victims at the hand of their own father. Besides the visitors at the door, they are the only other people singled out in the story. Perhaps it is these women, or women like them, who pray every night for God to intervene on their behalf.

SYSTEMS OF ROUTINIZED VIOLENCE are all around us, as close as the pages of the Bible I flip through to read of Sodom's destruction. In the fields where my grocery store produce is grown, countless low-wage and undocumented women are subjected to sexualized violence and rape. In some estimates, as many as 80 percent of all women in this line of work are victims of sexual harassment and intimidation.[1]

Picking is dangerous for field workers. From the apple fields of the Yakima Valley in Washington to the sweet potato fields of eastern North Carolina, many workers spend ten- to twelve-hour days in the sun, their eyes burned by pesticides. Workers have limited access to bathrooms and clean water. They are charged exorbitant prices for sodas, water, and transportation. Because they are often undocumented or in the United States on temporary worker visas, these people have little leverage in wage disputes. They become the victims of wage exploitation.

They are vulnerable to human trafficking and sexual harassment. The lack of protections for undocumented women, the isolation of fieldwork, and the drive for cheap food creates a system of abuse invisible to us during our weekly shopping trips to the local supermarket.

Marlyn Perez was one of these exploited workers. In 2011 her boss attempted to extort her, withholding her wages and offering her higher pay in exchange for sexual favors. In a secluded area of tall tomato plants, her harasser brandished a pistol after she rejected his advances.

These are common stories in the fields. "This entire industry was founded on a system of slaves, who were brought over and who suffered more greatly than we do even today," says Nely Rodriguez in an article for *The Atlantic*, in which she documents the exploitation of female field workers.[2] It's a system with roots extending through the immigration and food production systems, fueled by institutional sexism and racism.

Last year I read a letter authored by Alianza Nacional de Campesinas, a collective of farmworker women who endure the abuse of this system. In their open letter, I heard the cries of Lot's daughters, those lives bound up in systems of oppression. "We work in the shadows of society, in isolated fields and packinghouses that are out of sight and out of mind for most people in this country," the Campesinas explain. Addressing other women who are speaking out against their own experiences of sexualized violence, harassment, and exploitation, the women write:

> We understand the hurt, confusion, isolation and betrayal that you might feel. We also carry shame and fear resulting from this violence. It sits on our backs like oppressive weights. But, deep in our hearts we know that it is not

our fault. The only people at fault are the individuals who choose to abuse their power to harass, threaten and harm us, like they have harmed you.

In these moments of despair, and as you cope with scrutiny and criticism because you have bravely chosen to speak out against the harrowing acts that were committed against you, please know that you're not alone. We believe and stand with you.[3]

Scriptures like the story of Lot and Abraham in the city of Sodom remind me that the persistence of evil isn't always the act of individuals. We are caught up in structural oppression. We hear this echoed in the New Testament where we read that "our struggle is not against enemies of blood and flesh, but against the rulers, against the authorities, against the cosmic powers of this present darkness, against the spiritual forces of evil in the heavenly places" (Ephesians 6:12). Sexism, racism, and classism—these powerful forces work through human beings but are supported by ideologies and philosophies that operate within bureaucratic institutions and offices. In the Old Testament, we don't have the language of patriarchy or mass incarceration. Instead, the way the Bible helps us to understand systemic violence and oppression is through faceless crowds and nations, in cities like Sodom and Gomorrah.

IN *THE NEW JIM CROW*, Michelle Alexander opened the eyes of millions of people to the systemic racism of the United States prison industry. She showed us the facts. While the crime rate in the United States is below the international norm, the U.S. incarceration rate is six to ten times higher than that of other countries in the world. In an interview with *Frontline*, Alexander describes this as a "system of racial and social control."

Alexander roots this strategy in a backlash against the civil rights movement of the1960s. The "get tough on crime" mentality was woven of the same ideological racism as Jim Crow, the legal codes that enforced separation of black and white U.S. citizens following Reconstruction. These similar forms of systematic, racialized social control are at work in the United States today through the carceral system.

Alexander describes how, after decades of stabilized prison rates, the so-called War on Drugs led to a massive increase in incarceration, a shocking 600 percent growth between the mid-1970s and the year 2000. Millions of those incarcerated were black men. Today activists call our attention to the racialized difference in the way the current opioid epidemic, a drug dependence affecting primarily white communities, is being treated as compared to the crack epidemic of the 1980s and '90s. Anti-opioid campaigns are marked by compassion, calls for treatment, and attention to the devastation caused by addiction. The crack cocaine crisis that impacted many black communities was met with harsh prison sentences.

Jail time, writes Alexander, is only one piece of the degradation of black lives in the United States. Incarceration stretches out into communities of color, multiplying the destruction by denying ex-felons the right to vote and to serve on juries, relegating them "to a racially segregated and subordinate existence. . . . They are legally denied the ability to obtain employment, housing, and public benefits," writes Alexander, "much as African-Americans were once forced into segregated second-class citizenship in the Jim Crow era."[4]

In response, members of our church lead worship in prisons and protest outside them, as well as working with agencies that help women return to our communities after incarceration. It is no mistake that we are drawn to resist these institutions. They are the storehouses of social devastation in our community, especially in the lives of black and brown women and men.

Prisons are systems of punishment, systems that thrive on fear and money. Once, during a class I taught in a federal penitentiary, a student told me that he had become lost to himself inside—that incarceration stole his sense of self, his identity. He was stripped of his life, his family, and his career—everything that made up the fabric of his self-understanding. Reduced to a number and sentence, he became unmoored.

Those who emerge from prison return to communities that are also adrift. One day I spent hours on the phone fruitlessly searching for housing for an ex-offender and her teenage son. I knew that in our society this mother, wanting to start over again, would find the obstacles stacking around her, surrounding her, barricading her from what she and her son needed for survival. For the rest of her life she would check a box on job applications, marking her as a felon. She wouldn't be able to access food stamps, and getting her voting rights reinstated in North Carolina is a maze of frustration and dead ends. The son she left behind had lived for a decade without his mother. The trauma of incarceration extends in every direction, tentacles creeping their way into all parts of life.

The description of the Sodomites in Genesis 18–19 provides an image of these faceless systems and networks of oppression. They epitomize institutional power—a system enabled by people, yet a systemic power that cannot be reduced to individuals. Sodom is prison doors, green plastic trays, patdowns, expensive phone calls, lines of toddlers in the county jail waiting for their mothers during visiting hours. When Genesis describes seething crowds in Sodom, it is a caricature of evil. There's an absurdity to the description when we read that "the men of the city, the men of Sodom, both young and old, all the people to the last man" surround Lot's house to lay hands on his divine visitors (Genesis 19:4). We are meant to see a blur of faceless, nameless, manmade violence.

JUST AS QUICKLY as I want Sodom razed from the earth—to become a smudge of sulfur and ash—something is struck within me. It is the same chord, I imagine, that struck Abraham when he heard about God's plan to bring the cities of Sodom and Gomorrah to desolation. It's here, in Genesis 18, that we are offered a human picture of God, a story in which God decides to personally investigate the actions of the people of Sodom. God spends several verses in internal conversation, wondering if it's appropriate to tell Abraham about the coming destruction of the city.

But most significant in this story is that Abraham is able to turn God's attention to the individual people who live in Sodom. Abraham stands before the Lord as the visitors to his tent walk toward Sodom. He stands up to God, advocating on behalf of the city's inhabitants. What kind of God is this who will destroy the righteous alongside the wicked? The bargaining begins. Abraham pushes back.

If fifty righteous people live in the city, will God deliver them from this destruction? God thinks about it for a moment and relents. For the sake of the fifty, God will spare the city. Eventually Abraham whittles the number down to ten. Only ten righteous must remain in order for God to spare these cities. Yet, when God searches, not even ten are found.

I've needed this reminder of my failure to recognize my unwitting participation in systems of violence and oppression.

It's easy for me to exonerate myself from systemic oppression that seems so immense and unruly that I can hardly imagine another world outside of it. But the machine of sexual violence in Sodom tells me that my hands are not clean. Shrugging my shoulders at the enormity of the world's sin doesn't make me righteous. I am as guilty as the rest.

Reading narratives like Sodom and Gomorrah, I attempt my holy discipline of being disturbed by the right things. I let the text upend my own sleepy complicity. In both explicit and implicit ways I benefit from centuries of racialized oppression that has given my forebears access to loans, homes, and property denied to people of color. I benefit from educational access and neighborhoods that lack pollution and crime. I benefit from a country that was founded for my flourishing. I benefit from a world of whiteness.

Because of this I pause in Genesis 19, with my own anger at God's willingness to save Lot. For all of Lot's offers of hospitality and protection of his visitors, he does not bat an eye as he offers up his daughters to be raped by the crowd of men scratching at his door. If there is a system of sexualized violence at work within the city of Sodom, Lot is part and parcel of its inner workings.

Still, God intervenes on behalf of Lot, which, for me, is a frustrating twist to the story. In Genesis 19, the visitors to Sodom hurriedly guide Lot, his wife, and their two daughters out of the doomed city. Lot's character is made no more attractive by his unwillingness to depart from Sodom. He dawdles through the morning before being taken by the hand and pulled out by the visitors who tell him to run and never look back. He quibbles over the place they should seek shelter,

cowering in fear, second-guessing and questioning those who
have come to save him from death.

Why does Lot want to stay? Why does his wife look back
at the charred remains of their city? Perhaps getting by in
Sodom—learning how to navigate the social order, how to
thrive in this system of oppression—has worked out well for
Lot and his wife. Perhaps Lot and his nameless wife resist leaving because they, too, benefit from figuring out how to work
within the confines of abusive power.

In sifting through Genesis 19, I come to discover the difficult truth that the character with whom I most identify is
the unfortunate wife of Lot. It may seem arbitrary and cruel
that, so close to freedom, Lot's wife looks back at Sodom and
is turned to a pillar of salt. We receive no other information
about what transpires, just this one chilling line about her fate.

But I recognize myself here. I see myself looking back in
longing at what I have known, trusting that it's better for me
to take my chances in benefiting from bureaucratic and institutional oppression than in forging a new world. I remember
Lot's wife when the idea of working toward a different social
order seems frightening and impossible within the crushing
grip of power that animates our world. I am no stranger to
looking back at the survival I have managed to carve out
within white supremacy, and every time I am turned to salt.

Lot: the one saved by grace. His wife: the one who cannot
tear herself away from the old world. I need both these stories
because they are both true within my own life. At different
times in life I have found myself in both of them as I work
to figure out how the people of God should live. I remember
that Lot is not saved because of his upright moral character
but because of a gratuitous act of God's mercy. "So the men

seized him and his wife and his two daughters by the hand, the Lord being merciful to him," we read in Genesis 19:16, "and they brought him out and left him outside the city." God was merciful to Lot, and Lot was in need of mercy.

It is Abraham who believes that others besides Lot could be freed from their participation in the systemic oppression of Sodom. Abraham, in his negotiations for the righteous in Sodom, was affected by a strain of mercy similar to what God exercises toward Lot. Mercy sees within the crowd breaking down Lot's door some who could be redeemed, pulled out from the wreckage—those who could repent from and resist the systemic violence that subsumed the inhabitants of Sodom.

I wonder if this is because Abraham knows what it's like to be called out, to be set apart from a people, from a nation, drawn into a new life and way of being. I wonder if Abraham knows another life is possible for some of the people in Sodom because he has seen firsthand how God can make a way out of no way, life out of death, a people out of no people. God has done this for Abraham, calling him from all the nations of earth as he and Sarah become the first seed of God's people. I wonder if Abraham's spark of compassion is lit because he knows that a person can be given a new name.

HARRY PANGEMANAN sits on a pew in the Reformed Church of Highland Park, New Jersey. In the newspaper photo he looks weary and shocked. For the time being, this will be Harry's new home, the stained glass windows and the chancel his living room.

A week earlier, Harry was awarded the 2018 Dr. Martin Luther King Jr. Humanitarian Award from the Highland Park

Human Relations Commission. For six years Harry led teams of volunteers to renovate homes devastated by Superstorm Sandy. He entered the United States on a temporary visa in 2012, fleeing from Indonesia. When asked why he decided to overstay his visa, he explains his fears about being a Christian in a country where recently a Christian governor was sentenced to two years in prison for blaspheming the Qur'an.

One morning after returning home from driving his daughters to school, Harry saw a black SUV with tinted windows outside his home. Fearing it was Immigration and Customs Enforcement (ICE), he locked himself in the house. Then Harry called his pastor, who picked him up and drove him to the church. Harry entered into sanctuary at Reformed Church of Highland Park.

For decades, churches have been places of sanctuary for those fighting deportation. In the 1980s, churches around the country opened their doors to immigrants escaping political and social unrest in Central America. Churches are able to provide sanctuary because of a memo directing ICE agents to avoid arresting undocumented person in "sensitive locations." These included medical facilities, schools, and religious communities. It's a loophole, a tentative and fragile way for churches to create extra time while lawyers work toward a stay of deportation for their clients.

My friend Amos is the associate pastor of Reformed Church of Highland Park, and I've often wondered if our time studying John Calvin and Karl Barth at Princeton Seminary prepared him for the work of housing an Indonesian refugee in his church basement. I'm grateful to hear Amos's words as I listened to a recording of the sermon he preached the week after ICE agents sought to detain and deport his parishioner.

ICE agents are deeply feared among immigrant communities. They are part of systems of control and enforcement, given orders they obey without regard to their moral turpitude: orders that separate mothers from children, orders that rip apart communities and friends. To those who are on the other side of ICE raids, these arrests are kidnappings. Loved ones are disappeared, perhaps never to be seen again.

I have no doubt that these are the fears and terrors that overshadow those facing deportation in Highland Park. As Amos tells me, immigrant people there wonder how they can live their lives without "being hunted and haunted." So it was with some surprise that I heard Amos's sermon end with hope for the redemption of ICE agents.

"Madness, cruelty, evil": Amos pulled no punches as he preached about the racial profiling and white nationalism that grips our immigration system. For my friend, ICE agents are part of a powerful system that is described in the New Testament through stories about demons. According to the people who lived at the time of Jesus, supernatural forces are at work in the social and economic frameworks of the world. People knew what it meant, Amos preached, "to be oppressed and possessed." The work of our lives as Christians, he told the congregation, is to exorcise these demons in ourselves, our churches, and our country.

Our work is also to set free the bodies and minds of ICE agents who are possessed by the inhumanity of our current immigration practices. His voice wavering, Amos preached, "I hope and pray that these confrontations will bring ICE field officers to a point of revulsion, wailing, sadness, and regret as the unclean spirit leaves their bodies, at which point we will help them up and embrace them back into the healing community of a restored humanity."

Later that week I call Amos to check in with him. Across many state lines, Amos and I find that in both testaments of the Bible, we're finding the same God working in the same ways. God is intervening in human catastrophe, coming down into human life, breaking apart systems, loosing those who have been led to believe that this is the way things must be, freeing those who cannot see their own participation as contributing to the terror of their neighbors. Perhaps God, in God's unknowable mercy, will reach down and take them by the hand, and rescue them.

Amos preached his sermon on an exorcism in Mark 1. In this gospel story, Jesus travels to Capernaum to preach in the synagogue, and there he is met by a man convulsing with an unclean spirit. The man cries out: "What have you to do with us, Jesus of Nazareth? Have you come to destroy us?" (Mark 1:24). The answer is "yes." God comes to earth to destroy the seething masses outside Lot's door, the demons invading the bodies of the vulnerable. The story sounds familiar.

In both the Old and New Testaments, we are released from sin as an individual problem, a personal act of repentance and transformation. That kind of redemption is present in our Bible, and it matters. But it stands alongside narratives that help us to see sin as corporate and endemic, a system from which we cannot escape, one from which we must be set free by a merciful God. Like Sodom, our world holds evil we cannot extricate ourselves from, oppression that lives in our blood. Only God can open our eyes, help us to see, and lead us to a new people, a new future, and a new world.

Perhaps even I can be saved.

4
GOD OF MEMORY

Remember what Amalek did to you on your journey out of
Egypt, how he attacked you on the way, when you were faint
and weary, and struck down all who lagged behind you; he did
not fear God. Therefore when the LORD *your God has given you*
rest from all your enemies on every hand, in the land that the
LORD *your God is giving you as an inheritance to possess, you*
shall blot out the remembrance of Amalek from under heaven;
do not forget.
   —DEUTERONOMY 25:17-19

Did he think I would fail to remember myself?
   —JULIA KASDORF, *THE BODY AND THE BOOK*

While I would timidly venture to bring the destruction of
Sodom and Gomorrah to my congregation, I have never
preached about the Amalekites from the pulpit. I can imagine
the wide eyes and the ashen faces staring back at me. I know
that my pastoral constitution is to want to clean up the violence, to justify God or those who misheard God. I'd like to
let texts like these be subsumed into the loving arms of the

New Testament's portrayal of God as Jesus Christ. I want to alleviate the terror of these words for my people when I preach our Scriptures.

I love preaching, but the reality of our Christian tradition of proclamation is that we carefully cut around the edges of our Scriptures, clipping them out of their place within the wide narrative arc of the biblical story. At the Islamic school in my city, the young students not only study the Qur'an but work toward its memorization. They are formed for a discipline of encountering the text as a whole, able to recite their holy writ for hour after hour. The Christian tradition in which I was raised was more interested in picking out individual verses to commit to memory. Plucked from context and narrative, these words could be wielded in whatever way we desired.

For the Jewish community, the story of Amalek is swept into the long story of God's faithfulness to Israel, the complicated choosing of a king, the protection of God's people against their enemies, and the internal tensions of stories, prophecies, and teachings of compassion and forgiveness that directly contradict commands like the kind given to Saul to wipe out the Amalekites. Earlier readers, our foremothers and fathers, show us how to live within the broad reach of the Bible.

In reading the entire story, we also learn that Amalek is the descendant of Esau, the brother of Jacob. As I began to grapple with what this could mean for my reading, I felt a strange sense of gratefulness mixed in with my discomfort. The redactors of the Bible—those who followed after the wisdom of the Holy Spirit in piecing together the Bible before us today—kept this story in its place. In the same way that Sodom reminds us of the need for a God who comes to the aid of those enmeshed in systemic evil, the Amalekites complicate my desire for vengeance. When I read this story within the narrative of Esau and Jacob, I come to acknowledge that others have been wrong when they hear God's words, and that, in spite of it all, God is in the business of turning all things toward good.

MANY OF US who live in economically rich parts of the Western and Northern hemispheres read the Bible today without the kinds of enemies that ancient communities knew. Their world was blood and retribution, rape and slaughter. We can imagine, if we try, what it must have been like to read that God was *for* you: for your life in the face of powerful enemies who ruthlessly sought out the lives of you and your children.

When the prophet Samuel declares God's word of judgment against Amalek, the Israelites receive the command as a reassurance that God is for them, that God has taken their side against the Amalekites. And early Jewish communities turned to this story as they sorted through their longing for vengeance, rummaged through the rubble of their burnt-out homes, and searched for the bodies of their murdered loved ones. Did the call of wrath upon babies, innocent of the crimes of their forebears, give these communities pause? Did they remember another call for the destruction of a city called Sodom, and how the leader of their people at that time, Abraham, asked God to relent?

What if we stay for a while with these ancient readers, lingering here instead of turning away? Perhaps we will discover that the discomfort welling up in us comes from God creating space for us to see ourselves here—these stories exposing our own vengeful desires, our own fears mirrored in the text. What

will I do in God's name? Do I want to read Scripture as war-
rant to punish people, as permission to make someone's life
vile? How will I hear God's punishing?

The Bible tells the story of God and humankind—stories
about us that are narratives about God, stories about God
that are narratives about us, each enfolded into the other,
inseparably bound together in a single volume. From page
to page, book to book, chapter to chapter, we encounter
the human and divine in the same verse, the same ink, as
one bleeds into the other. To discern who we are learning
about in this or that passage demands careful attention,
contemplative patience. When we are reading, the text blurs,
the subject of the plot shifts in the mystery of the story. "Is
this about God or about us?" we wonder. "Does this narrative tell us what God thinks about God or about what a
human character in the story thinks about God? And is that
person in the story right?"

The story of the Amalekites presses into these questions.
The people born of Amalek wander through the Old Testament. They are a people whom generations of interpreters
have charged with moral turpitude, a filthy and disgusting
people. They are said to be such an infectious curse that the
Bible records God's call to eradicate them from the earth. The
Amalekites hold an exceptional place in the Old Testament.
No other people in the Bible are looked upon with such loath-
ing, no other people assigned a permanent place of dishonor,
generation after generation.

The Old Testament records the Amalekites' multiple
attempts at plundering the Israelites. "Remember what Amalek did to you on your journey out of Egypt, how he attacked
you on the way, when you were faint and weary, and struck

down all who lagged behind you; he did not fear God," we read in Deuteronomy 25. "Therefore when the Lord your God has given you rest from all your enemies on every hand, in the land that the Lord your God is giving you as an inheritance to possess, you shall blot out the remembrance of Amalek from under heaven; do not forget" (Deuteronomy 25:17-19).

Moses speaks these words to his people—his voice outlining God's law for Israel. What do we learn about Moses here? What do we learn about the desire of his people—the pastoral words they need to hear, given their experience of persecution, their long struggle to stay alive after redemption from Egypt, their struggle for survival in the wilderness? And what do such words and desires reveal about God?

The story of the Amalekites takes us deep into the landscape of Israel's generational trauma, far into the country of human enmity, grief, and terror. Amalek is Israel's persistent enemy. The Amalekites provide an explanation for the irrational and intense hatred for Jews that echoes through human history. In Jewish history the Amalekites—a tribe with genocidal intentions against God's people—came to symbolize all those who sought to eradicate the Jewish people, from Titus to Hadrian, Khmelnitsky to Hitler. The interpretive work for the rabbis was to explain how the command to curse Amalek by blotting out his line forever had been fulfilled through the death of Haman in the book of Esther. Israel was no longer under obligation to enact physical vengeance upon an extant people. Amalek remained as a metaphor, lurking in human history as a persistent force of evil.

One of the most painful narratives about Amalek preserved in the Old Testament is found in 1 Samuel, where the prophet Samuel declares to King Saul. "Thus says the LORD of hosts,

'I will punish the Amalekites for what they did in opposing the Israelites when they came up out of Egypt. Now go and attack Amalek, and utterly destroy all that they have; do not spare them, but kill both man and woman, child and infant, ox and sheep, camel and donkey'" (1 Samuel 15:2-3). Saul carries out the command, but only in part. He preserves everything of economic value, along with the Amalekite king, Agag. "All that was despised and worthless they utterly destroyed" (1 Samuel 15:9).

It may seem precarious to say these are the words of a people traumatized, the memories spoken down through every generation to remind the people that they are not alone. It might seem troubling to hear that while this is God's Word, these may not be God's words. After all, what will keep us from erasing the pages of the Bible that aren't to our liking? Thomas Jefferson famously took scissors to the Bible in one such attempt at cleaning up the Scripture.

But it's a different disposition to look back at the Bible as a record of God's interweaving with human life. It's different to see that there is something for us here, in the text—truth in the words. These stories call us to a form of remembering that we, too, pass down, each time we open these pages of the Bible. Each time we read, we explore our fear, our enmity, and our vengeance. These stories are preserved in our Scriptures because we find God here.

The Old Testament theologian Walter Brueggemann once said that God is a recovering practitioner of violence.[1] But perhaps instead it is us—those who read these stories—who discover a startling truth about ourselves in Scripture.

Enemies are real. There are destructive forces of violence that haunt the lives of the vulnerable. Like in the story of

Sodom, we need a God who names evil, a God who is on the side of those oppressed and forgotten. But this acknowledgment is not meant to be done in the isolation of this or that narrative. Our questions are meant to stretch across biblical stories, carried from generation to generation by all of us as we work out our relationship to God and our neighbors.

Our Scriptures provide scripts for how to read these relationships—the Bible as a wealth of narratives that invite us to position ourselves as characters within the stories, to feel our way into God's life. That's what we experience as we wrestle with Amalek and the Amalekites. And as we involve ourselves in those stories, we are drawn into family history, a family feud.

To know the story of the Amalekites, we have to tell the story of the father of Amalek, a relative to Israel's family. We have to know the story of Jacob's brother, Esau.

I HAVE A PENCHANT for biblical losers. The Old Testament is in the habit of unsettling our piety through these marginalized characters. They frustrate supposedly clear lines that separate those who are in from those who are out. The story of Esau and the nations birthed through Esau's offspring offer a tender and frustrating tale of ambiguous prophecies that change destinies, prophetic words that introduce us to a God who works toward the good of all.

Before Esau and his twin Jacob are born, their futures escape their control. "The elder shall serve the younger"; "one shall be stronger than the other" (Genesis 25:23). Imagine what it must have been like: Your mother whispering words over your crib, your body curled next to that of your twin brother. Imagine what it must have been like, hearing the women talking as the two of you walked along. Imagine as they told you, Jacob, the story of how you grasped at your twin's foot—you, The Grasper, always at his heel.

"Two nations are in your womb, and two peoples born of you shall be divided" (Genesis 25:23). With this announcement, God appears to Rebecca. She has gone through a season of barrenness, a strange condition for the woman who was prophesied to carry on the line of God's chosen people. Now not one but two nations wrestle within her body, until she can bear it no longer. Brothers are born, twins who are distinct yet the same, who will strive against one another for the rest of their lives. Their struggle will reverberate through time, all the way to those of us who call these Scriptures our own today. Their intertwined, diverging, and reconnecting lives will birth a child named Amalek.

In the birth story of Jacob and Esau, we find ourselves in a strange position. It is difficult to stand back from the text, because we know where the story ends. It is Jacob through whom the promise will extend, Jacob through whom God's people will flourish. And it is through Jacob's line that Jesus comes into the world. "Abraham begat Isaac, Isaac begat Jacob, Jacob begat Judah and his brothers," we read in Matthew's gospel (Matthew 1:2).

If we can find our way back, reading without this ending in sight, we can see that the story's outcome is thorny, that the relationships are woven together, inseparable—brothers returning to one another even as they attempt to unravel.

After the initial prophecy to Rebecca and the jockeying in the womb, the twins grow up together. Over time the differences between them blossom. Esau: the red one, hairy and strong, beloved of his father, a hunter in the field. Jacob: the grasper, sly and zealous, dear to his mother, living in the tents.

One day Esau returns from a hunt famished, ready to eat anything. Jacob offers him stew in exchange for his birthright, and, strange as it may seem, Esau takes the bait. The terms are switched: Esau will have one-third of his father's inheritance while Jacob takes the rest.

In this story no one comes out looking good. It's ambiguous, a muddle of fear and failure, ambition and anxiety. Jacob is no hero. He's a plotting usurper, taking advantage of his brother at a vulnerable moment. Jacob envisions the expansion of property and wealth as implicit in God's promise. He sees an opportunity and grasps at it.

Esau, on the other hand, comes across as bumbling and oafish, a hungry, animal-like teenager who makes bad decisions. He's impulsive and coarse. But at no point does the Bible apply a moral judgment to either of the twins. They aren't described as evil, nor are their actions condoned by God. They act very much like people.

While we get no clear moral judgment out of this story, we do discover in Jacob and Esau a caution about trying to make the world work out the way we think God intends it to be.

IF WE LINGER on those haunting words spoken by God to Rebecca during her pregnancy—"two nations are in your womb, and two peoples born of you shall be divided"—we find that there's no indication of how this will work itself out. The prophecy is ambiguous, the words in Hebrew unclear. Ultimately, we decide, as readers, who will serve whom as the plot develops—as Esau and Jacob jostle with each other, fighting for their own version of the prophecy, scrambling for a future in which one beats the other. We are like Rebecca and Jacob, deciding and plotting for themselves which child will be the victor. Similarly, we read into the story who we believe the winner will be. And in our reading we contribute to the catastrophe.

According to Rebecca's intention, God has chosen her favorite child, Jacob, to carry on God's covenant. And Jacob knows the course this usually takes: inheritance, lineage, power, money, a name. It's a promise, one that Jacob plans to follow through with steadfast devotion. Jacob is bent on fulfilling this single purpose, and willing to do whatever it takes to make it come about.

The breaking point for Esau and Jacob comes when the twins' father, Isaac, is on his deathbed. In addition to passing down the birthright—the physical inheritance of land and property—the father will place a blessing on each of his children. In a reenactment of the scene of that meaty stew traded for the birthright, Jacob disguises himself as his brother and tricks his old, blind father into giving away Esau's blessing. Esau cries out, "Have you only have one blessing, father? Bless me, me also, father!" (Genesis 27:38). Isaac places his hand on Esau and tells him these are the only words left for him:

> See, away from the fatness of the earth shall your home be,
>   and away from the dew of heaven on high.
> By your sword you shall live,
>   and you shall serve your brother;
>   but when you break loose,
>   you shall break his yoke from your neck.
> (Genesis 27:39-40)

Esau pledges to kill his twin in retaliation.

Yet this isn't where the story ends. These lives will not be separated. They weave in and out, bearing the consequences of the past while being drawn toward one another. After exile and separation, Esau and Jacob are reunited. Jacob sees his brother again, as if for the first time. He looks on his twin and says, "seeing you is like seeing the face of God" (Genesis 33:10).

After years living under the consequence of deceit, Esau and Jacob are reunited. Here is what Jacob says to his brother, "Please accept the blessing that was brought to you, for God has been gracious to me and I have all I need" (Genesis 33:11). Jacob has discovered the truth of God, a God he encountered at Bethel, making a way between heaven and earth, a God who wrestled Jacob to the ground and marked him for life. "I have all I need." Jacob cannot undo all the violence he inflicted upon his brother, but he gives what he can—a replica of the gifts of the birthright inheritance intended by their father. And in the end what was taken is returned to its rightful recipient. The blessing intended for Esau is repaid.[2]

We read this passage in the same way it is lived out, as a story about winners and losers, the chosen and the rejected. But all the time God is there in the ruins, showing these brothers that there is enough, enough blessing for all, enough love for all, enough of everything. It isn't simply that God disrupts social formulas and lines of inheritance; God does it in such a way as to work towards restoration.

Maybe the story of Jacob and Esau gives us a chance to see that God's sovereignty, God's ability to move in the world, can coexist with us being wrong. Maybe this story helps us to see that God's sovereign work is also to undo our wrongness, to undo us. When we think we know what God intends, when we hear words we believe are God's, we could be wrong. We could follow these words to our devastation, but even then God is in the work of redemption.

Maybe Jacob and Rebecca were wrong. Maybe Isaac, the father of the twins, who lived to see his own brother Ishmael blessed, to see God take the knife from his father Abraham's hand—maybe Isaac over his long life learned to see this other possibility, the hope found in having enough for two blessings. Isaac learned it in his own life and lived out this lesson for his sons.

Jacob spends the rest of his life undoing what he had done. He spends the rest of his life returning the blessing of property and goods, what was intended by his father, what he stole, back to Esau. And that's how God works in the world. God turns us around, back towards redemption. God sets things right—not just in the end, but all along the way, even when the terms we set for good and evil bring about disaster.

FROM THE PROGENY of Jacob and Esau arise the enemies and allies that dot the stories of the Old Testament. Among Esau's offspring is Amalek, the thirteenth son born to Esau and his nameless concubine.

The Amalekites are both foreign and same, known and unknown. They are the siblings of the Hebrew people, the same blood running in their veins, the same brothers binding them together. When the call comes to blot out the memory of Amalek, it is not a call to destroy an outsider. This is an internal struggle, a working out of enmity within a people. Whenever we hear the stories of Amalek, of God's call to "blot them out," this other story—the story of Esau—lingers in the background. It nags at us, reminding us that these, too, are our brothers. The story of Esau ends in blessing; the story of Amalek ends with a call to eradication. What we discover about the character of God is that both stories are allowed to co-exist.

Enemies are real. They must be named for the brokenness they inflict. And we may also find that these enemies are closer to us than we care to imagine.

In the book of Exodus there is a curious phrase about the Amalekites that reminds us that these lost siblings will always be within us: "Write this down in the memory-book and set it before Joshua: I will blot out the memory of Amalek forever" (Exodus 17:14). This passage contains the historical memory of how the Amalekites appear as enemies of Israel in the Bible, a story planted at the foot of the Promised Land.

My memory, like all our memories, is scattered. It's a path along which I have erased certain markers, while in other places I have built towers out of what were likely only small piles of rocks. In the same way, in the memory book of the Bible, we see the markers set along the way, built by memories like mine, the memories of all of us. We can retrace our steps, encountering again the rocky places and the smooth valleys. I suppose Israel is like that too, finding that our memories both change and change us. Maybe these words are meant to be remembered for the work they do on us, each generation of Israel, from age to age.

And in the memory book of Israel, the command from God to blot out Amalek was written down as a marker. These words are read each year in synagogues on the Sabbath before Purim. Each time these words are read, Amalek is remembered, undoing our forgetting. There is something here that God wants us to remember. Perhaps Amalek gives us time to puzzle over the catastrophes of our enemies and our interconnectedness to them. Perhaps we are meant to wonder for a moment about our vengeance, to call to mind Esau, and to remember that God is setting all things right, often in spite of us.

We carry the story of Amalek alongside others, with Esau, with Moses, with those who recite these words and hold up the memories of others who have watched their people led to slaughter. We work out within us our own capacity to break open the world with violence, to take God's words and turn them into our own, to have them undone again before us.

Esau and Jacob let us see that we explore the nature of God and ourselves when we read the Bible. We find our words in God's mouth and God's words in ours. We are working out who we are and who we think God is along the way, in the long faithfulness that is reading the Bible. This Bible is a discovery of God through human lives, a story that scatters signposts of memory showing us the way home again, putting out lights so we can see the path illumined. We get lost; we find our way back. The way is there, waiting.

The trouble is that we are usually in a rush to make sense, to pull out the stories of Old Testament violence and hold them up for judgment, because we are not entirely sure we want them to be ours. We are not convinced we want this God to claim us. I suspect we want something easier: a plain text, a God who stands outside and above us, setting up morally clear judgments for all time. Instead, we get questions. What will we hear? What will we believe? What will we live?

BECAUSE THE CHURCH has most often made an enemy of Esau, it is difficult to find images of this ancestor in faith. I searched in vain for an image of Esau until I came across an icon commissioned by Pax Christi, a Roman Catholic organization that works for the end of warfare. The center panel of the icon shows the twins, Esau and Jacob. In 1999, Pax Christi's international assembly was held in two locations in the Middle East—Amman, Jordan, and Jerusalem. These are lands where the blood of Jacob and Esau's warring nations drenched the land.

The icon was written at the monastery of St. John in the Desert. In the top panel Esau, dressed in red to symbolize humanity, embraces Jacob, robed in the blue of the divine. Their faces touch, the cheek of Esau pressed into his brother's face. Their eyes are open.

We can imagine that the writer had in mind the moment when Esau and Jacob are reunited, when Jacob proclaims that seeing his brother is "like seeing the face of God." The icon depicts motion, the movement of the brothers. Although they are not yet embracing, they appear as if only a step away from doing so. The sword from Esau's sheath is on the ground. The brothers together stand on it, rendering it useless.

In the background, propped against the rock, is a ladder. We are meant to recall the ladder Jacob saw in a dream, after his deception led him into exile, away from everything he knew. On this ladder he saw angels, ascending and descending from heaven. Here again we discover that the line between God and people is unclear. We see the place where God's life is complicated within the story of people, and we are there, observing it all.

Without stories about Jacob and Esau and their descendant Amalek it would be difficult for me to take the Bible seriously. The Old Testament would be colorless religious platitude idealizing heroes and villains. Instead, the Bible makes room for terror and hope, for what is possible and what is not. We are shown the far edges of enmity and our fear is exposed. And here Amalek holds a space for the complication of that enmity as we discover the enemy within us, how the Bible calls for each generation not to forget.

God of Wanderers

*Jacob left Beer-sheba and went towards Haran. He came to a
certain place and stayed there for the night, because the sun had
set. Taking one of the stones of the place, he put it under his
head and lay down in that place. And he dreamed that there was
a ladder set up on the earth, the top of it reaching to heaven.*
  —GENESIS 28:10-12

*There is a spirit that pervades everything, that is capable of
powerful song and radiant movement, and that moves in and
out of the mind.*
  —PAULA GUNN ALLEN, *THE SACRED HOOP*

Last week I came early to set up our worship space. It was
silent and still in the empty room that would transform into
our sanctuary. I unstacked the metal chairs one by one, turning their angle slightly toward the center so that those who
gathered for worship could see each other around the table. I
placed the table in the middle of the room, drawing us near to
the bread and the cup.

Setting up and taking down are two of the rituals I love about church, and I'm grateful when I get to participate in them, to invite the possibility of holy space. I am afforded this small pleasure because our church rents its space from a school. During the week the place where we worship on Sunday mornings is crowded with girls and boys who play catch and eat lunch, study on folding tables and sing in assemblies. The walls of our shared room are covered in superheroes and inspirational quotes.

When I come into the quiet space, I am reminded of all the places where Christians worshiped over time: in basements and upper rooms, in catacombs and caves, around kitchen tables and gold altars. Those places became holy spaces because people met God there—a God always on the move and unpredictable, an unknowable God made known.

In the Old Testament, God's presence and God's elusiveness are in tension. We hear this pull in the vow Jacob makes to God after he wakes from a dream and sees a ladder connecting the heavens and the earth, and angels on the ladder, descending and ascending:

> "If God will be with me, and will keep me in this way that I go, and will give me bread to eat and clothing to wear, so that I come again to my father's house in peace, then the Lord shall be my God, and this stone, which I have set up for a pillar, shall be God's house; and of all that you give me I will surely give one tenth to you" (Genesis 28:20-22).

Jacob will build a house for God, a place where God's spirit can dwell. At the same time, he wants God to go with him, to follow him on the way, to assure a way of peace before him. I suppose much of human life is reflected in Jacob's dilemma—torn between wanting a God who is free and one who will stay in a holy place.

As it is, sometimes I expect God to show up at my invitation: in church where I organize the chairs, set up a lectern, and light candles. And other times I'm surprised, even afraid, because God shows up in places where I think (or hope) God should stay away. Genesis 28 is testimony to my discomfort. Most translations of this passage say that Jacob "came to a certain place" on the road, a stop along the way (Genesis 28:11). Wording with more feeling behind it would say that Jacob "collided with a place." He slammed into it. The rabbis elevate this interpretation by explaining that Jacob was caught off guard by the coming night, because God had turned up the clock and caused the sun to set early. He had to arrange a campsite quickly, before nightfall. It was this place that overtook Jacob. At times we are overtaken by a place where God shows up.

The rabbis understood the nomenclature of God's name and the word *place* to be the same. And when the rabbis hear these verses from Genesis 28, they determine that in this story we discover that there is no place without God, that all places where God appears are holy places.

THROUGHOUT TIME the church has been tempted to bring about and control holiness, to expect that we can make God show up. Often we believed that places were marked as holy by our naming them as such. We think we are owed this as God's people.

The building where my church worships each week sits on the land of the Sappony and Cherokee, the Lumbee and the Coharie. We are the occupiers of this land because of laws that made it available to colonizers, laws rooted in the Doctrine of Discovery. This doctrine provided the spiritual and theological underpinning for the European conquest of what we now call the Americas. We find the logic of this principle laced throughout the Western church's declarations. In "The Legal Battle and Spiritual War against the Native People," published in 1493, Pope Alexander VI writes, "Among other works well pleasing to the Divine Majesty and cherished of our heart, this assuredly ranks highest, that in our times especially the Catholic faith and the Christian religion be exalted and be everywhere increased and spread, that the health of souls be cared for and that barbarous nations be overthrown and brought to the faith itself."[1]

The pope's administration goes on to describe how the lands on which our church meets today are "empty lands," vast swaths of territory without inhabitants. The indigenous peoples who live here, their bodies rooted into the land for generations, are merely occupants of God's lands. Native peoples who did not cultivate and harness and exploit this ground in the same manner as the European elite were not taking proper advantage of God's good gift. As such, Alexander VI argued, non-Christians had no claims to this land. Whatever lands were "discovered" by European explorers were the colonizers' to conquer.

The next five hundred years of policies that removed indigenous people from their lands, that gave legal advantage to settlers, had roots in the Doctrine of Discovery. To the present, this Christian logic led to the murder and displacement of millions of native women, men, and children. Their cultures were eradicated, and both their trauma and their resilience echoes for generations, down to the present.

The theological claim undergirding all of this is that a holy people are called to lay claim to lands marked and waiting for colonial arrival, waiting to be taken up by the blessed. The land itself is blessed, holds within it a holiness that is for us, God's chosen. The European colonists saw the Old Testament justifying this claim, from Abraham to Isaac to Jacob to Joshua. They saw God's people being called out of nothingness for the purpose of taking hold of the land promised to them, a land where Canaanites dwelled, and there establishing themselves. God's people, many of the stories in Genesis, Exodus, and Joshua explain, would displace these peoples, erasing them from history.

But the Old Testament holds out other stories for us alongside narratives of claiming holy land. These other stories remind us of the wildness of God, the untamableness of God's life, and the unpredictability of God's blessing. The duality of God's permanence and freedom is made visible in the transition from the tabernacle—the impermanent structure where God's spirit dwelled in the desert wanderings—to the temple, the ornate building constructed in Israel's new home, in Jerusalem.

I empathize with the longing for permanence that the people of Israel felt. I feel it within myself. If I mark and claim holy space, maybe God will stay put. And if I set up a place, a permanent place, set down a rock, give it a name—if I do this, then I'll know where to find God when I decide I want God to show up. If I make a temple, I know where to go back to find God. Often it's a rude awakening to discover that God thwarts my plans for stability. The priests who dedicate the newly constructed temple, initiating God's presence among the Israelites, remind me I am not alone.

I am going along, minding my business, and God disrupts things. This plotline has been a fixture throughout my life as I stumble into a place I did not expect to be. Because of this, I furrow my brow in knowing solidarity as I read about the priests of Solomon's temple in their encounter with the surprising and overwhelming presence of God as recorded in 2 Chronicles 7. The priests have put together an incredible celebration following a seven-year-long building project. They're moving God from the tabernacle, a tent that has traveled with the people, into the solid structure of the temple. It's moving day for God.

The priests throw a huge party. They organize a parade where they march the ark of the covenant into the temple. These holy butchers sacrifice so many sheep and goats that they cannot be counted. The temple is beautiful, with gold and angels and precious stones everywhere, set against deep-colored tapestries.

At first we think, "It's a success!" God shows up! The priests were able to do it. A cloud fills the house of the Lord, reminding us of the cloud that led the people by day as they wandered in the wilderness after escaping Egypt, the fire by night. Textbook temple-consecration.

But it's not quite what they expected. God *really* shows up. We read that the whole temple is filled with a cloud so massive, so unexpected, that the priests have to stop what they're doing: "They could not stand to minister because of the cloud" (1 Kings 8:11).

One of the common threads in the Old Testament is that humans frequently find ourselves trying to domesticate God. People want God to show up, but almost always on our own terms. How could we expect otherwise? While we may think of death, violence, and destruction as a kind of interruption, in reality this is more or less standard fare. We are on a consistent trajectory of things going wrong, for ourselves, our loved ones, and our world. In the church we call this original sin, which is another way to say that we are assaulted by and conspirators with death-working powers from which we cannot disentangle ourselves.

It was no different in the days of Solomon than it is now. War, violence, the oppression of the weakest, political instability, death—all of it circled around the people like vultures in the sky. But in the midst of it, God was there. God went before and behind them—a cloud by day and fire by night. God was in their midst, making a way. And eventually it was time to settle God down in the place where they lived, with their king. Our forebears in faith longed for a world where God provided reassurances and consistency with the same intensity as the chaos that swirled around them.

But that isn't the way it is for God. God doesn't clean up after our mess of human frailty and cruelty like some cosmic janitor. And God doesn't provide reassurances for whatever ruling family happens to control the space assigned for God's holiness. Those are human answers, what people can imagine as a way to interrupt the terrors of this world. More often than not, our human attempts to secure God for ourselves have catastrophic consequences, as they did in the Americas.

Instead, God is always getting away. We encounter a God who is free, who spills over whatever dam we have erected to channel God's presence at the appropriate rate and within the bounds of what we think we can handle. God is in the business of disruption, of getting underneath what orders the chaos of sin and death. God takes our petty solutions and washes them away.

At the dedication of the temple, Solomon talks about God showing up like a thick, dark cloud. When God shows up in this way, it's usually to remind the people that God isn't another object to be harnessed or controlled. There's an edge of danger to the story, this God who will not be contained in the appointed space.

This God-who-gets-away also assures me that I am not worshiping something of my own creation, an utterly miserable pursuit. In my honest moments I will confess that I prefer a God who gives out prizes for good public behavior, for acts of justice and mercy. I'd prefer a God who is slightly less concerned about my internal workings, particularly the bit about coveting the many shiny things in the world I would like to call my own. I'd prefer a God who blasts evil from the earth without the slow tedium of this redeeming-all-things business.

But this God, the rumbling cloud that sends the priests running from the temple—this God keeps showing up, keeps surprising me, keeps making new ways where there is no way, keeps saying yes to a world that is mean and ugly. This way of holiness is infuriating at times; it is always unnerving and often unruly.

IT HELPS that I am not asked to believe any of this on my own, but that others with their flesh and blood followed this untamable God in their own untamable lives. In some churches we call these people saints—women and men who brought unease to kings, popes, and religious leaders. Because we're Mennonites, my church has a rather loose definition of sainthood. Even crabby Aunt Bea is remembered as someone who passed down some bit of wisdom or fortitude to those in her life. These saints, curmudgeonly or otherwise, have left for us the stories of their encounters with the cloud of dangerous holiness that kept showing up.

On a Sunday when we remember those who teach us about the persistence of God's unruliness, I light a candle on our worship table for Etty Hillesum, a Dutch Jew who lived and died during World War II.[2] In reading her journals, I learned that she had the chance to stay in Amsterdam but felt a strange call growing within her. She explains that she wanted to draw near to the fate of her people, those being taken to concentration camps, taken to death.[3] She left Amsterdam and spent time in a transit camp, where she was able to bear witness, offering support and steadfastness, knowing her life as a Jew was imperiled.

Hillesum taught me many things through her journals. In one important life lesson she explains, "one must not try to take stock of one's life at one's most tired and weary moments, lest one become unnecessarily sad."[4] I now live by this sage advice. But beyond these bits of cheeky wisdom from the diaries she kept from 1941 to 1943, her pages of reflections reveal her growing awareness of God's care for her as her months in the Westerbork transit camp stretched on. Hillesum saw faces passing through on their way to death, her people, and in each one of them a fragile piece of God.

There was nothing to do, nothing except to bear witness to God's continuing presence among a people slowly being extinguished by evil. Her journals are remarkable. As horror and terror grow, Etty Hillesum is moved closer and closer to God. With no religious training, and nothing in the forms of piety we often use to mark someone as saintly, she was there, observant of God's expansive and wild presence, a woman who, in the valley of the shadow of death, revealed God's life to others.

Eventually she was packed on to a train and taken to Auschwitz, where she died in a gas chamber along with her whole family. On the train she took a postcard, a pen, and a Bible. Opening at random she put her finger down on these words: "The Lord is a strong tower." She scribbled the words on the back of the postcard and flung it to a friend as the train ferried her to her execution.

Hillesum stands among those who have brought me to this day by showing me the way of an unmanageable God. When we talk about this "great cloud of witnesses" who uphold us and sustain us, they too bear within them an edge of danger. Their lives remind me of the thick fog that sends the priests running from the temple, the place colliding into Jacob where God unexpectedly shows up—wild, uncontrollable. When we find ourselves among these saints, we encounter a world spilling over with God. We encounter a God who cannot be contained, even by death.

LIKE THE PRIESTS in the temple, Jacob stops at Bethel to be encountered by God, and there he discovers that God will not be controlled, that the sky can part and the curtain between the heavens and earth be ripped in two. And he is filled with fear. God can show up anywhere, when you least expect it, when you aren't ready.

For those who settled the land where I worship each Sunday, it was easy to assign God's holiness, to attach it to people and places. As I think about what that means for me, the ways my ancestors, early colonists to this land, marked these lands as holy, I feel anxious bringing up a past we cannot alter. Guilt about the past has the power to make it impossible for us to move forward. We find ourselves paralyzed by shame.

But reckoning with our past, seeing how our Scriptures have been used for both devastation and for blessing—this can help us to live differently into the future as we embody practices, policies, and habits that rechannel our desire to control God. The Bible is consistently a story of humans making sense of God's redemptive action in the world while at the same time wrestling with our desire to control God, to make God do our bidding, to make God into our image.

What we learn from Jacob at Bethel and the priests of the temple is that God will not be conjured for our protection, our victory, or our economic stability. Jacob learns this on the way, interrupted on his journey, slamming into God at the in-between place. The priests learn it as God's presence overwhelms them with mystery. We learn to show up in the dark, at our most vulnerable, exposed to the possibility of God.

As time went by, the Hebrews grew more insistent upon God's mediating, place-based presence. Bethel—the place Jacob names where God meets him along the way— becomes a place of security, a place of calling down God and reassuring God's people of their chosenness. And, as people do, they utilize this chosenness not to be a blessing to all nations but instead for destruction, for oppression. Centuries later the words of the prophet Amos will ring out across the land:

> Seek me and live; but do not seek Bethel,
>   and do not enter into Gilgal
>   or cross over to Beer-sheba;
> for Gilgal shall surely go into exile,
>   and Bethel shall come to nothing. (Amos 5:4-5)

Over and over the prophet's words burn: Seek the Lord. Seek good and not evil. The chosenness of Israel is the gift of a loving God, and the holy places of Gilgal and Bethel have instead become idols of assurance, a way to claim that God tolerates the rich preying on the poor. Amos' words burn:

> Therefore, because you trample on the poor
>   and take from them levies of grain,
> you have built houses of hewn stone,
>   but you shall not live in them;
> you have planted pleasant vineyards,
>   but you shall not drink their wine.
> For I know how many are your transgressions,
>   and how great are your sins—
> you who afflict the righteous, who take a bribe,
>   and push aside the needy in the gate.
> Therefore the prudent will keep silent in such a time;
>   for it is an evil time. (Amos 5:11-13)

Amos reminds us that a place is holy because God shows up there, because our lives are an invitation for God to be present. We wait with hope. All that we can do is issue an invitation. God has met us here before. Perhaps God will meet us here again.

WHEREVER GOD'S SELF is made firm in human life, we encounter the holy. And so it is that every so often members of our church pack a car with balloons, soda, shampoo bottles, coloring books, and a giant purple cake. With these items we've collected, we drive two miles to the women's correctional facility. There we host a party for twenty of the incarcerated women whose birthdays fall within the calendar month we are celebrating.

The bright orange flowers and neon tablecloths stand in stark contrast to the flat gray walls of the prison dining room.

We set the tables with care, waiting for the women to file in, their names checked off against a list by a correctional officer. When they arrive, we go around the room to introduce everyone, asking each of the women about her favorite birthday memory. Many of the women share that they can't remember a birthday celebration that was just for them. Others recall bittersweet memories of the birth of a child from whom they are now separated. Some talk about an early memory, a time before life got hard and complicated, a time when the world wasn't roll call and mopping the dining hall.

We go on to sing "Happy Birthday" and serve each of the women cake and chips. We play rounds of bingo and charades, distributing shampoo, conditioner, and beef jerky to the winners. We laugh and talk, refilling cups with soda, all under the watchful eye of two prison staff members.

At the end, when our time is up, we form a circle. "Would it be all right if we held hands?" one of the women asks. We gather close, holding tightly to the people next to us. Around the circle we say a wish, remembering when we were little, when we made a wish while blowing out candles on a cake.

"I want to celebrate my next birthday anywhere but here."

"I hope no one else in my family dies before I get out."

"I want to be a good mother, to go home to my children."

"I want to be a grandmother to my grandchildren again."

"I want to be somewhere else."

"I wish to be brave here."

Wishes like a prayer, the sky opening up, our hands a circle of grief and hope. And just like that God shows up in the stuffy cafeteria of a women's prison. We slam into a holy place.

We mark the place not with a stone but with words. Looking into each woman's eyes in turn, I say one of our ancient blessings, a blessing often said when we discover holiness is happening around us. These are words given to Aaron, the first priest—words handed down on the lips of saints, generation after generation. They are words to mark a people as beloved. "So they shall put my name on the Israelites, and I will bless them," God tells Moses (Numbers 6:27).

My words are an invisible mark on each of the women as I say the blessing again: "The Lord bless you and keep you; the Lord make his face to shine upon you and be gracious to you, the Lord lift up his countenance upon you and give you peace" (Numbers 6:24-26).

"Do not go to Bethel," Amos warns. Holiness marks the land, marks people unexpectedly, without warning. The land is holy because God shows up, because the sky parts, for a moment a ladder connects earth and sky, land below and heaven above, because at any moment and in any place God finds us where we are, evading our grasp, and yet always with us, to the very end.

6

God of Darkness

He uncovers the deeps out of darkness,
and brings deep darkness to light.
   —JOB 12:22

Faith sees best in the dark.
   —SOREN KIERKEGAARD, *UPBUILDING DISCOURSES IN*
   VARIOUS SPIRITS

It is not my constitution to wake in the middle of the night, but one night in late spring I set my alarm for 2:00 a.m. Groggy, I shift a blanket around my shoulders and shuffle down the hall to my daughter's room. I gather her against my chest and whisper, "It's time."

We go out to the concrete slab that leads into our backyard. The warm heat of the day has given way to an unexpected cool here in the middle of the night. My daughter sits on my lap in a rickety lawn chair, staring at the sky. We wait for stars to fall.

We are not alone, sitting in the dark, waiting for something to happen. In Deuteronomy the gifts are so close, springing up around us, finding their way to us even when we are not looking. But it isn't always like that. The Old Testament makes space for the broad reach of human life. And it gives holy space for the dark.

Darkness is the main character in the story of Job. Following a divine wager, Job is moored to a life with no children, his home destroyed and his body racked by disease. Evoking the day he was born, Job shouts, "Let the day be darkness!" "May God above not seek it, or life shine on it," he weeps to his friends. "Let gloom and deep darkness claim it. Let clouds settle upon it; let the blackness of the day terrify" (Job 3:5).

"I read the book of Job last night—I don't think God comes well out of it," Virginia Woolf writes in a letter to a friend.[1] The God of Job keeps us on edge. This God is twice trapped into a divine wager with Satan, making a game of a faithful servant's life. We wonder about God's ability to act justly as God devastates Job's life without cause. If the point is to prove that humans will continue to worship God without reward, it is a nasty and tragic bet.

It's understandable that for the upright Job, darkness is everywhere—circling around his eyes, blocking his way, the color of a bed made within a grave. Job is unsettled by the dark. It is no friend: "He has walled up my way so that I cannot pass, and he has set darkness upon my paths" (Job 19:8). Job doesn't fear the dark; he is lost in it. The God he knew has disappeared into the shadows; the God he worshipped is gone. Job searches around for new names for God and finds them: enemy, jailer, hunter, spy (13:24, 27; 19:8; 7:20).

This is not the type of story we typically level at children, but one year I stumbled upon a rare opportunity to learn from Job alongside one of our church's younger members. Every year my church participates in Children's Sabbath, a worship service dreamt up by the people at the Children's Defense Fund. Communities of worship from around the country invite children to take on the entirety of the service—reading Scripture, ushering, displaying art, and leading in prayer.

While my church regularly put together a meaningful Children's Sabbath, preaching remained firmly in the hands of adults. One year I wanted to try something different. I wanted to give a child in our congregation access to the pulpit.

Because I am brave or foolish, or because the line between the two is very thin, I decided to continue our practice of centering worship on the Scriptures from the lectionary rather than picking out a child-friendly story. I discovered that the passages for the next four weeks were all from the book of Job.

I asked a nine-year-old named Hannah if she was interested in preaching. Hannah is naturally curious, a quality I value in a good preacher. She loves church and she's not afraid. I remember one Sunday after Hannah read Scripture from the pulpit for the first time, she turned to her mother and said, "I have been waiting my whole life to get up there."

In her living room, while her mother prepared a snack of apple slices, Hannah and I read aloud the first chapters of Job. Paragraph by paragraph, we encountered oozing sores, piles of trash, heaps of ashes, dead offspring crushed under the weight of a felled ceiling. After we were done she turned to me and said, "I don't think this story is appropriate for children."

But we forged ahead into the work. We wrote a sermon together. And what Hannah determined was that God doesn't do well at being God in this story. God acts like a person, she told me. It's Job who never gives up, who stays faithful, who sits in the depths of his pain—literally in ashes—but does not stray from the path of love. God, the one up in the clouds, peers down, unaware and unmoved by Job's disintegrating life. This God is erratic, easily tricked, led away from faithfulness. Hannah told me that we want a God like Job. It's Job who acts like God, the way we want God to be for us.

I admit: I was anxious about this reading because I'm a pastor. These honest questions, these devastating questions about God's behavior—these questions make me uncomfortable. I'm not always sure how to do justice to these deep terrors in the short space of a sermon. It is my tendency to keep God in the light, where I can decide what to make of the divine. I work against an innate desire to come to God's defense. But Hannah would have none of that. We had lost hold of the God we'd come to expect.

Hannah is right. Almost all of us worship a God of *quid pro quo*, a God of retribution and wagers, a God who rewards good behavior and politeness. With Job we awaken in the middle of the night and the God we have come to expect has disappeared.

In the chapters leading up to God's reemergence, Job is confronted by a variety of companions working on the same plane of logic and with the same expectation of God. Thirty-seven grueling chapters into the story, God's character is still eerie unknowability. But then something changes. God appears in a tempest. Gone is the God of cosmic games, hovering above the earth. Instead, God begins to speak poems about God's work within the intricate details of earth's operation, mapping owl migrations and storing up rainwater.

"The great question that God's speech out of the whirlwind poses for Job and every other person of integrity is this: Can you love what you do not control?" writes the biblical scholar

Ellen Davis. A God of checks and balances, one who rewards and punishes along the predictable lines of ethics—this God is predictable. We can shape ourselves around this God, setting up our disappointments and wins according to schedule. But a God who counts newborn deer, a God who is concerned with eagle nesting patterns, a God who lassos sea monsters—this is a God we cannot regulate.

And as God takes on a new, unknown, unpredictable form, darkness is transformed. God speaks from a whirlwind of darkness to Job's despair. Throughout his long chapters of speeches and rebuttals to his friends, Job's descriptions of darkness are brimming with pathos. His words for darkness communicate death and despair. But here at the end, God reveals to Job that darkness is not chaos. Darkness is held, formed, and purposed, placed into an ordered and complex world. For Job, darkness is separation and death. For God, darkness is another facet of a created world, a world not immune from death but also full of God's sustaining and ordering care.

To put a point on the matter, God's speech to Job begins with a frank question: "Who is this that darkens counsel by words without knowledge?" (Job 38:2). The darkness of which Job has spoken dozens of times is not coming as a threat from the outside, closing in on him. The darkness is within Job, spilling from his mouth.

I KNOW JOB'S TERROR. For years as a child I was afraid of the dark. In defense of my life against what I believed were unseen and unnatural entities roaming under my bed, waiting for a chance to attack, I would quickly turn off the light on my nightstand and yank my hand under the covers as fast as I could. Like many children, I had a strange intuition that light could not protect me from whatever unseen things emerged into my room in the night. I hid, sweltering, under heavy blankets. Only a deeper darkness could keep me safe from that which crept in the light of my imagination.

Job cannot fathom that darkness holds a promise. And into this despair, God offers Job a tender and disarming image. It comes as one of a long series of questions hurtled toward a presumably stunned Job. "Who shut in the sea with doors when it burst out from the womb?—when I made the clouds its garment, and thick darkness its swaddling band?" God thunders (Job 38:8-9). God relays to Job the story of the infant sea bursting from the womb, then wrapped in bands of darkness to comfort it and keep it still. Darkness is a blanket, tightly gathering in a newborn child. Darkness is comfort, comfort at the gift of losing the God of our own making.

In the crushing night, Job, who cries out against darkness dozens of times, finds the night defused. Rather than forces of violence, or odes to inescapable pain, the darkness and light become beings with dwelling places, personas who come and go, creatures who are ushered in and sent away again. Job fears the crouching dark, but even darkness has its place.

Job's struggle with darkness echoes in other Scriptures. One of the most disturbing and descriptive accounts of darkness in the Old Testament is found in Psalm 88. "Are your wonders known in the darkness, or your saving help in the land of forgetfulness?" the psalmist asks (Psalm 88:12). The God the psalmist seeks is hidden, a purveyor of wrath and dread. Unlike almost all other psalms of lament, this psalm makes no attempt at a tidy ending, provides no assurance of the constant fidelity of God. When I hear the final line of Psalm 88, I imagine this prayer in the mouth of Job. The final chilling words are whispered into the silence: "darkness is my closest companion."

Darkness and light are the language of the eyes. And as I hold this psalm close, as I let its sorrow work over me, I begin to wonder about places where there is only darkness. The deepest place on earth is the Challenger Deep in the Mariana Trench, almost seven miles below the surface of the water off the coast of Japan. It's a mile taller than Mount Everest. If I dropped a stone from the water's surface, it would take it over an hour to settle to the bottom.

When scientists wanted to establish a baseline for oceanic noise, they went to the Mariana Trench and recorded for twenty-three days. They expected to find only vast swaths of silence. Instead, they discovered sounds of another world. No light penetrates these depths. But sound does. The recordings are preserved for the public. On a scratchy soundtrack, I can hear the low hum of a baleen whale passing more than 1,000 feet above the sound equipment. A minute later an earthquake rumbles past. Listeners hear ships' propellers and the noise of oceanic traffic.

After listening to the recordings, a friend and I discussed the virtues of sound over sight. We remembered hearing of theologians who suggest that sound provides a truer metaphor for understanding what our encounter with God is like. That makes sense to me. In seeing, we're able to choose what we see. We can avert our eyes, miss something, focus on what we want to see. But for those of us with access to both visual and auditory senses, hearing renders us vulnerable. There is no getting out of hearing. We cannot escape sound, even in the dark.

When God answers Job "from the whirlwind," it is an approach from speech, God's presence as the sound of a dark storm. God speaks, shouts, hurls words toward Job. Job's God must first be lost in darkness and found there again.

JOB TAUGHT ME to love the dark, and to love what I might find there. I imagine this is why I am always ready when the hinge of the year swings open the door to Advent, the season in the church devoted to waiting in darkness.

One of the gifts of growing up in a liturgical tradition is that my life has been marked by the rhythm of church time. I know that Advent is waiting for me. Before Christmas, and often in the face of mind-numbing consumption, Advent makes room for the dark. In this season, we find ourselves like Job. We let ourselves lose the God we've come to expect, to keep watch, and to see what comes in the night. Advent is the time when we stay awake, readying ourselves for the discomfort of encountering new names, of letting the God we thought we knew fade into obscurity.

The morning after twenty first-graders were shot and killed in Newtown, Connecticut, I picked up the *New York Times* to see their faces, mirrors of my own seven-year-old child's face, staring back. Advent was there to receive my terror. Another year in November, Tamir Rice, a baby-faced twelve-year-old, became the next in a long line of black men, women, and children who have died at the hands of police. Advent cradled my weeping congregation as we wondered about this God who allows the death of children to persist unabated and unpunished. That year Advent led us into the streets, our fists lifted to the night.

The season of waiting in the dark sets the path that leads us into Christmas, where almost all the significant stories of the nativity are shrouded from the light. Here in the dark shepherds will tend their flocks. Here in the dark magi will gather for escape from King Herod. In the warm cave of Mary's womb a baby gestates. In the dark Mary will awaken with a new feeling, a tension rippling up her swollen belly as she wonders, "Is it time?" In the cover of darkness a family will flee to Egypt. And here, in the dark, a man stays alert in the night, waiting for a thief.

It is not surprising that we begin each new liturgical year where we ended the year before. We begin with an apocalypse, a disclosure, a revelation. But instead of a thing brought to light, we discover that we are feeling our way through a dark room, our hands around the outline of something we do not understand. We are doing our best to feel for the edges, to get a sense of where we are, of who we are, of the God we discover along the way. We're asked to wait a while longer.

The lectionary begins Advent with the "little apocalypse" near the end of Matthew's gospel:

> But about that day and hour no one knows, neither the angels of heaven, nor the Son, but only the Father. For as the days of Noah were, so will be the coming of the Son of Man. For as in those days before the flood they were eating and drinking, marrying and giving in marriage, until the day Noah entered the ark, and they knew nothing until the flood came and swept them all away, so too will be the coming of the Son of Man. Then two will be in the field; one will be taken and one will be left. Two women will be grinding meal together; one will be taken and one will be left. Keep awake therefore, for you do not know on what day your Lord is coming. But understand this: if the owner of the house had known in what part of the night the thief was coming, he would have stayed awake and would not have let his house be broken into. Therefore you also must be ready, for the Son of Man is coming at an unexpected hour (Matthew 24:36-44).

It's a dizzying, confusing description, filled with passive verbs. Early in my life as a Christian, I was instructed with intense clarity as to the particular persons in history who were identified in this story, who was in and who was out. But now I know that the objects of the verbs in this passage are unclear. There's a cryptic reference to the few saved alongside Noah, the others swept into the flood. We hear that two will be in a field, one taken and one left. Two will be milling grain, one taken and one left.

The language is strange. Is the one taken saved? Or taken into the flood? The one left—is she spared from death, or does she remain on a desolate earth? How can we find ourselves within this confusion, not knowing whether we are staying alert to leave or to remain?

And what happens to the one who waits up for the thief? Is the owner's presence enough to frighten him away? Does he confront the thief, fight him off? Or does he recognize that he isn't a thief at all but a friend? Does the owner invite the thief in?

One late night my daughter and I were walking back to a cabin in the woods, having left our flashlights behind. My daughter shivered near me as the trees swayed and sighed high above us. She was afraid. Something could be out there waiting for us, ready to pounce in the shadows. "Or maybe," I told her, "we are being hidden by the dark, kept safe." It was impossible to say. We stayed close together, taking small, careful steps.

As we walked, I remembered the night when my labor for her began. As I swayed through waves of pain, my heavy belly tensing through contractions, my midwife told me stories of the babies she had watched be born. "Of hundreds of births," she told me, "all but three labors began in the night." She mused that deep within women is an instinctual sense that daylight makes us vulnerable to predators and marauders. The last thing a woman wants is to find herself unable to retreat from danger for several immobile, child-birthing hours. Night is a cloak, hiding us from death as new life is birthed.

The ambiguity of Matthew's prophecy of the thief makes it difficult to know if in darkness we are hidden or hunted. Because of this, we find we cannot align ourselves with end-time winners or put ourselves on the side of the righteous. We don't have enough information. There's too much unknown, too much confusion. Instead we're asked to sit with the owner of the house, ready for the unexpected to greet us at any time. We are called to a readiness of patient attention to the unknown, without having it all worked out for us, without being able to stake a claim. We are asked to press deeper into the disorientation of the text.

The ancient rabbis believed the Messiah would come in the night. Perhaps that was because darkness offers to disorient our senses, because in darkness we cannot help but see things in a different way. We make room for the impossible in the space made by the dark. In darkness we're not entirely sure who is standing on the stoop, picking at the lock—whether this one is here to help or to harm, to kill or to comfort.

In Matthew's gospel we are drawn into the between time, when the owner of the house waits in the darkness after everyone else has gone to sleep, before the thief arrives. I'm drawn into those long, sleepy hours in which a man waits expectantly, as he gazes out into the night with nothing to be seen. We are there with him, shadows turning trees into sculptures or ghosts and the night turning friends into strangers. We learn the different shades of dark—how, even with no moon, we are still, miraculously, able to see.

If you have kept awake in the dark, then you know how different the world becomes, how the world at night is both strange and familiar at the same time. Barbara Brown Taylor reminds us that God puts out the lights to keep us safe "because we are never more in danger of stumbling than when we think we know where we are going."[2] Only when there are no more maps, no more compasses, no more lights to direct the way, are we fully vulnerable to God.

IN THE CHURCH'S HYMNODY, we are rarely offered darkness as an indicator of divine presence. This is a testimony to our embedded biases for metaphors of light as signs of God's grace. It was because of this absence that Brian Wren was commissioned to write a hymn that preserved the biblical weight of darkness. What resulted was the beautiful and eerie song "Joyful is the Dark." In one verse Wren describes the night cradling the dawn from which the resurrected Jesus will emerge from the tomb.

I have loved this hymn since it was first introduced to me in a church where I once worshiped regularly. We met for worship in the evening, and in the winter the light would fade around the chapel as we sang these words. The architect designed the chapel to reduce the space between the wooded trees outside and those who worshiped inside; he created a church of windows, vast panels of glass where full-sized trees shivered within view. On the shorter, colder days of the year, the night crept in around us. We would sing Wren's hymn about darkness roaring in thunderclouds, revealing divine depths, shrouding a majestic divinity. "Hallelujah! Sing and tell the story," we proclaimed in one voice. I could feel God's words from Job—a darkness wrapped in swaddling bands as the night pulled us closer, held us within and without.

On those nights when the warmth of darkness enveloped our worship, our voices in unison singing of the majestic deep, I pulled up the memory of my child, heavy on my chest, waiting for a meteor shower. It is night that offers us space to set aside the God we have created and to see what emerges, like stars falling, like the world falling apart. Like Job, we lose the God we thought we knew in the night. Then we wait to see what happens next.

7

GOD OF WONDER

When you have come into the land that the LORD your God is giving you as an inheritance to possess, and you possess it, and settle in it, you shall take some of the first of all the fruit of the ground, which you harvest from the land that the LORD your God is giving you, and you shall put it in a basket and go to the place that the LORD your God will choose as a dwelling for his name.

 —DEUTERONOMY 26:1-2

The answer must be, I think, that beauty and grace are performed whether or not we will or sense them. The least we can do is try to be there.

 —ANNIE DILLARD, *PILGRIM AT TINKER CREEK*

My daughter and I are huddled close, squeezed into the corner of the crowded coffee shop down the street from our house. Our hands are curled around paper cups of hot chocolate. I read in my low voice, trying not to disturb the bleary-eyed students hunched over laptops and textbooks.

Flora and Ulysses is Kate DiCamillo's story of a superhero squirrel who writes poetry. I am a bit embarrassed at how moved I am by this children's book. I hide the quiver in my voice by clearing my throat. The pages of my seven-year-old daughter's book are worn, fanning out on the table as I thumb to the place where I begin to read aloud. She leans in, her eyes on her cup.

We are in the middle of this story about Ulysses, a squirrel who is supercharged by an unfortunate encounter with a vacuum cleaner. Of the many abilities that result, the most auspicious is that he writes poetry. Ulysses pecks out several exquisite lines of poetry at the typewriter, to the utter amazement of Flora, his human companion.

Flora's surprise arises from the miraculous exposition of a literate squirrel. But she is also astonished to be noticed, and even more surprised to become the object of someone else's delight. Flora lives largely overlooked in her world.

Each time I read one of the chapters, Ulysses reminds me to give my attention. Ulysses notices, and he is filled with wonder. He's confronted by the beauty of the world, sometimes by the overwhelming fragility and feeling of the world. "What is the word for that?" he asks. Is there a word for the lighted windows of other houses? Is there a word for how his human friend, Flora, looks when she sleeps? For the wind blowing through the trees, or for a donut with sprinkles on top and cream on the inside? Or jelly, maybe?

These are the questions I can imagine God asking in the midst of setting down a celebration of first fruits. It's a ritual of belovedness. Deuteronomy tells the story of this celebration of the first round of grapes, the first shivering stalks of wheat. "When you have come into the land that the Lord your God is giving you, as an inheritance to possess, and you possess it, and settle in it," the commandment in Deuteronomy reads, "you shall take some of the first of all the fruit of the ground, which you harvest from the land that the Lord your God is giving you, and you shall put it in a basket and go to the place that the Lord your God will choose as a dwelling for his name" (Deuteronomy 26:1-2).

Here in Deuteronomy we discover a people in a desert, a generation lost to wandering in the wilderness. And we learn that they will eventually be led into a green place. God will make a way for them. And they will encounter beautiful things. Everywhere they look they will come up against this loveliness. They are about to enter a world of contrasts with the death-dealing of the desert. This new world is brimming with life. In Deuteronomy we learn that God notices it too. God wants the people to delight in what is around them.

It is one thing to notice the beauty of the world. It is something else to delight in what we notice. When the rabbis imagine the basket for the offering of first fruits in Deuteronomy 26, they imagine delight. They write that the basket at the altar included sweet things: milk and dates, honey and pomegranates.[1] It has always struck me that in the rabbinic imagination, the first fruit offerings were not limited to staples like flour for bread. The people are not asked to lift up only that which ensures survival, but the excess, the extravagance of the land.

The first fruits point back to God's abundant, profligate goodness as the gifts fall into the hands of God's people, as the people look them over in wonder. In Deuteronomy God notices and God delights in the texture and smell and feel of this world. God asks the people to go into the land and to bring it near, a little bit of all of it.

What does it mean for us to worship a God who wants something like this to happen, a recognition of God's good and perfect gifts, a feast expounded upon in Deuteronomy 16? The festival of first fruits is to be carried out by Israel continuously, every three years, forever. What does it tell us about God that God wants this—that God excitedly draws people to grapes and honey, the quotidian surprise that every year the harvest will come again?

We worship a God who wants us to see the world, to taste it, to love it and delight in it. We are in good company when we find others who love what we have found in the world in this way, those who have loved the world for itself, and have found themselves confronted by the wonder of it.

To know the world as God knows it is to give our attention to the sound of gravel kicked across concrete, the stutter of light through the guardrail as cars pass on the other side of the highway, the sound of an oboe, the warmth of a piece of bread pressed into your palm.

God notices. God loves creation for itself, puts it here with no other purpose than to be lovely, for us to delight in it. And in Deuteronomy God points people to all these lovely things. "See," we imagine God saying, "Look and see! Taste, touch, and see."

IF YOU ARE SEARCHING for the epitome of passion and fervor, look no further than the person who runs the children's section of a bookstore. Not long ago I stopped by our local bookstore to pick up an order for myself and decided it might be nice to buy something for my middle child. After wandering around for a while, I enlisted the help of the woman who runs the children's section.

She spent twenty minutes taking me from shelf to shelf. Each book was an exclamation, a story that fit into her own life or the lives of her sons, her descriptions a pure act of delight. At one point, when I had nearly seven books in my arms, she passed by a hardcover volume with the picture of an old Harlem brownstone on the front. "I have to tell you about this one," she said, "even though it won't work for your six-year-old." And she wove together the story for me: the family who lived in this house, redemption for the lonely man who lived on the upper floor, the unexpected gift of the new family that was created. Soon I realized she was crying, dabbing her eyes with a tissue.

The woman at the bookstore reminded me of another story in our Scriptures. In the gospel of John, Mary comes to Jesus to anoint his feet (John 12:1-8). Like most women in John's gospel, the women are more in tune with Jesus' ministry than his male followers, more aware of who he is. With this knowing, Mary comes to anoint Jesus for death, an extravagant act in which she pours perfume on Jesus' feet. It's absurd in its worth, and Mary is met with censure by Judas. "Why was this perfume not sold for three hundred denarii and the money given to the poor?" he complains (12:5).

As Jesus watched the perfume dripping from his feet, Mary gently wiping his feet with her own hair, I am reminded that the most beloved in the offering of first fruits are those who appear before the altar with their gifts. They are the unnamed gift of the celebration. All are invited to this feast: the children and the sick, the widows and the aliens. They are all beloved, all partakers of the goodness of the land. In this moment, their lives are grafted together.

And at this moment the people, the new arrivals to this land of promise, will recite their history. They are told to speak it back to God, to tell the story to one another. "*We were a wandering people, who became great in Egypt, afflicted and abused and enslaved,*" Deuteronomy 26 tells them to recite. We can imagine them looking at one another, mothers to sons, neighbors to friends, and saying, "*God rescued us. God brought us up, brought us to safety and to abundance, to the land of these dates, brought us to these trees, to this hill, to this grass, to the fruit in my hand*" (my paraphrase). "Look," another translation could read, "look at it right here" (Deuteronomy 26:10).

The feast of remembering first fruits, mentioned in Exodus 23:16 and again in Leviticus 23:34 as the Feast of Tabernacles, is when God instructs the people to tell back the story of their past. It's a shock to discover that there are significant pieces left out of the words they are told to recite in Deuteronomy 26, gaps in the narrative of their past. Important historical details are omitted from the record. Most notably, there is no mention of disobedience, or complaining in the wilderness, and not a word about wandering for forty years or about Moses hitting a rock for water—no mention of the distrust and disloyalty, the failure and death. There's nothing said of the Ten Commandments. No description of golden calves and broken tablets. Not a breath spent on promises made and kept and broken. No responsibility. No getting better, being more faithful, following the rules. Not a word of any of this.

Dorothy Day begins her autobiography, *A Long Loneliness*, with these words: "When one writes the story of his life and the work he has been engaged in, it is a confession in a way," she explains. "When I wrote the story of my conversion twelve years ago I left out all of my sins but told of all the things that had brought me to God, all the beautiful things, all the remembrances of God that had haunted me, pursued me over the years." She writes that it is difficult to do that "without a ritual, without a body with which to love and move, love and praise."[2]

In the feast of first fruits God gives the people a ritual of noticing and awe. God gives the people words to say, words about wonder and grace. And God has left out the parts about their sin. They simply are not remembered here. It is as if that is left behind, there in the dry heat of the desert. Once a year everything else is pushed aside, and all that remain are the wonders.

COMMUNION IS LIKE THIS TOO, an ingathering of our gifts and our bodies, these good things returning back to us, making a way to our lives. I have often marveled at how God chose to pass on Jesus' body to us through a meal. God could have called our attention to the horror of crucifixion by having us pass around a cup of vinegar. Jesus could have told us to remember him among us by saying some words or holding silent meditation. Instead we are given something to eat— fellowship around bread and a cup. Sweetness and warmth. "This is my body, for you."

In a church where I once worshiped, we would share monthly meals, sitting ourselves on folding chairs around tables in the basement. Here the pastor would begin with the words to bless our communion. "On the night that he was betrayed Jesus took the bread. In the same way he took the cup." Those words bounced across Jell-O salad, swirled around ham sandwiches, hovered above Dixie cups of lemonade. "Whenever you eat this bread and drink this cup, whenever the gift appears, whenever you gather together, I am with you." Whenever it happens, wherever it happens, Jesus is remembered.

As it was for Israel, so it will be for those of us grafted into Israel, Gentiles welcomed into God's encompassing promise to all of creation made known in Jesus Christ. For Israel, in the time to come there will be death and covenants, promises broken and promises kept, but mostly promises broken. There will be exile and war, sins that follow kings and priests and children for generations.

That is for another day. Here, in the children of Israel's body, in the ritual of first fruits, the people receive the good news of a God who gives them back the memory of their belovedness.

Remarkably, this celebration gathers together the aliens and Levites alongside those who own the land. They are all included, all welcomed to partake. Those who pray and those who work, those who own land and those who live by the mercy of others—all of them are invited to receive the first fruits at the altar. The whole community becomes a gift, a living embodiment of the diverse gifts placed in the basket.

The words that initiate this celebration of first fruits are a reminder of the source of this expansive giving. God's people were set free from Egypt, redeemed from the oppression and violence, but also liberated into a new land.

The celebration is miraculous because people are endlessly frustrating. I do not hold up my end of the bargain and neither do you. I am doing less work while you are doing more. There's a leveling that happens at the celebration, one that breaks out in this ingathering celebration. The one who plants and waters and harvests receives the same as the beggar and the priest. The Levite and the alien share together around the table (Deuteronomy 26:11).

For a moment, everyone present at the feast remembers a common origin story. The feast of the first fruits is the fulfillment of the promise made when the people were freed from slavery in Egypt. "The Lord brought us out," they say (Deuteronomy 26:8)—everyone in the same boat, under the same whip, the same lash. Now we are here, noticing the same gifts as we watch God's grace unfold on every blade of grass, in every newborn calf.

AS IT IS, God is always calling our attention to gifts hidden in plain sight. And so it is that I slather my face in zombie makeup to perform Michael Jackson's *Thriller* dance before a crowd of two thousand people. Each year Reality Ministries puts on a talent show, and each year it grows, spilling out of its first location in an auditorium and now moving into this larger venue. The performers are people with intellectual disabilities and their friends.

It doesn't seem like the sort of thing that would pack out a performing arts center that typically holds crowds for *Wicked* and *Hamilton*. But tonight the seats are filled with people who have come to see an unusual performance.

Each of the talents is born from the joy of one of our disabled friends. We see their dreams put on flesh. One woman turns a fashion artist's drawings into real clothes, which three women with Down syndrome model on the runway. Another group forms a gospel choir, all of them in robes and swaying to the piano accompaniment. We hear a rendition of John Lennon's *Imagine*. One man reenacts the final challenge from *Who Wants to Be a Millionaire?*, complete with confetti meticulously cut and gathered for over a year by the young man who plays the game show host.

People with disabilities don't usually find themselves on a professional stage dancing *Soul Train* or performing the death scene in *Titanic*. Most of the time our friends are hidden from view, kept out of the way of a busy, productivity-obsessed world. The world moves fast, at a death-dealing pace, not enough time to see. We are not given the time to notice.

But we are all here tonight, and I am ready for our rendition of *Thriller,* ready to stand beside our friends on stage in my purple crepe dress because this was their dream. Their dreams are a gift, a profound act of noticing occasioned by making space in time. It's an unusual communion, the lives that intertwine through the talent show—an ingathering of a different sort.

God sets down these occasions for wonder, to notice the world, to notice God noticing the world. In the Old Testament, the noticing of the mundane and the taken-for-granted is ritualized as wonder. God puts them down on the path for us to come across them, in hopes that we will take them up, that we will hold before one another the gifts of our lives and discover that God has been delighting in us all along.

I think of the ritual of first fruits in our own home ritual of watching the garden. Each spring my son and I put our faces down in the garden beds, waiting and watching. Each sunny day we come out to stare into the dirt, to see if the first wisp of sweet pea shoot has emerged over night. "Anything yet?" he asks me, prodding a clod of earth.

It is never a guarantee, and we wait in hope. And when we see it, when the first thin tendril finally appears, it is as though we have experienced a miracle. Every year, no matter how often this small act of nature repeats itself, we receive it as a gift. How can something ordinary and expected bring such wonder? We dance around and whoop and holler. We take pictures of the growth, so small it looks silly on the screen of my phone. But we want others to see what we have seen. We want to share them, to announce to the world the wonders we've witnessed in our backyard. We want our friends to love these first fruits, too. We notice it all, and it is all beloved.

And this is how God feels about you, about each of us in this world. You don't have to be anything more than who you are for God to notice you, for God to give attention to the details of your life: the soft roundness of your head, the way your laugh starts with a burst. There is nothing you can do to be better than you are, no act of self-improvement, nothing you must accomplish to make yourself more useful to God or the world, nothing that would make you more beloved than you are right now.

You do not have to be braver or smarter or kinder or more faithful. You don't have to get over your fear or your sadness or your grief. You are enough, just as you are. You are God's first fruit. What is put before the altar is each of us, our lives, our beautiful bodies, each of us beloved of God.

In Deuteronomy, God calls the people to one another. A community is born where the poor and the rich, those with and those without, become participants in God's wonder. This people becomes a sign of God's wonder. God is the source of the wonder, but also the one to receive it, the one who gathers together this people. Each person reflects on this stunning mystery—we were aliens, too. We were despised, wounded, broken. God took us up, rescued us. God brought us here, to all of this, to one another.

I am still caught up in this awe as my daughter and I come to the end of *Flora and Ulysses*. The book finishes with a poem. It comes as Flora realizes, as all children must, that the road she walks is complicated by pain and sorrow. These are the words for her, the words of God to each of us written through the vehicle, as it were, of a superhero poet squirrel. "Nothing would be easier without you," Ulysses reminds the anxious child. She is everything. She is the sum total of the sublime and the ordinary. "You," writes Ulysses, as if God is speaking to each of us, "are the ever-expanding universe to me."[3]

8

GOD OF BIRDS

Even the sparrow finds a home,
 and the swallow a nest for herself,
 where she may lay her young,
at your altars, O LORD of hosts,
 my King and my God.
Happy are those who live in your house,
 ever singing your praise.
 —PSALM 84:3-4

The swallow has foresight because it goes out to fall and does
not seek the heights.
 —ISIDORE OF SEVILLE

After reading Psalm 84, I gave myself a special discipline for the week: to pay attention to birds.

For a week I waited and watched for them. I stood still by my window to observe the birds of my neighborhood. I stopped mid-conversation to see a bird on a picnic bench, tilting its head toward me. I waited in the long spaces where there were no birds and wondered at their absence. I scoured illustrations of speckled eggs and spackled nests meticulously drawn by patient hands. I leafed through photographs of grackles and cowbirds, nuthatches and waxwings, kinglets and larks, ibises and owls.

The memories of these birds came to me one morning as I sat in a pew during morning prayer at St. John's Abbey. A bird sang at the open door of the chancel just as we were beginning to chant the closing canticle. I looked around, expecting the tiny sparrow to alight on a prayer book, drawing its slender body to our worship. Instead, it stayed at a distance and we sang the psalm in unison. The bird's praise led us forth as we filed out through the bright silence of the day.

Another day I searched for birds in the pages of *The Saint John's Bible*, an illuminated manuscript written on vellum and embroidered with gold. It is a majestic and holy piece of art commissioned by the Benedictine monks of St. John's in the late 1990s. *The Saint John's Bible* is the first project of its kind since the invention of the printing press. Following the technique and discipline of early illuminated manuscripts, a collection of calligraphers and artists wrote and drew the ornate pages, the feathers of their quills twisting through the air.

The word *manuscript* means "written by hand," and because *The Saint John's Bible* is the labor of human hands, there are mistakes. Each page holds priceless resources and countless hours of work. When errors occurred, the artists had few options. Because of the expensive paper, ink, and time that went into every word, starting afresh was not one of them. Instead they followed the editing tradition of writers from centuries ago.

In early illuminated manuscripts, small errors remain on the page. These flaws were scratched out with a knife or polished away with pumice stone. But on occasion an entire phrase went missing. If the artist's eye inadvertently skipped over a line of the text she was copying, she inserted the absent words with a *signe-de-renvoi,* a "sign of return." This is a small symbol: two dots or a line, indicating the place of the transmission oversight. The absent line was then added in the margins designating where the reader should insert the absent text.

These signs fascinate me—the persistence of human error in the Bible, reminders of our fallibility. In *The Saint John's Bible,* human slipups are given greater attention. We are not to divert our eyes; instead, our attention is drawn to signs of human imperfection, embellishment of failure.

When I need to be reminded of my humanness, I will take out one of the reproductions of *The Saint John's Bible* and turn the tall pages to the gospel of Mark. In the margins a small gray bird ascends, clutching a blue string, hauling upward the words "could not even eat. When his family heard it they" (Mark 3:20-21). The bird's slender beak points to the place where the line belongs.

AT OTHER TIMES I've pulled out this picture to remind me that Steve is gone, an absence in our church, still fresh and strange. On these early Sundays since his death, it still catches me to remember that Steve won't show up to perch on the second seat of the fourth row on my right, listening for references to birds or angels or anything that might fly through the Scripture passages.

Steve was a pilot who used his life to find his way to those who are overlooked and abandoned, to make a way through the air to them. He died in a single-engine airplane crash on a routine flight, the only death on a warm December afternoon in an empty field in a rural North Carolina county. Steve worked to rehabilitate the local airport, an important injection of life into the local economy.

Steve was attentive to the fragility of creation, and he spent his free time flying supplies into Haiti after the earthquake, and to the Bahamas to build houses for people left behind by the tourism trade. Steve taught paraplegics how to fly. He believed in the future of women in aviation. But it was Steve's attention to animals in peril that always caught my ear when he told me stories of his latest adventures. I often thought of Steve as the little bird pulling forgotten words back to their rightful place in that illuminated manuscript, the overlooked finding their way back to where they belong.

Perhaps because of his time in the air, his time flying close to birds, Steve had a particular compassion for rescuing animals. One year Steve was contacted by a local animal rights organization in West Virginia. They had been alerted to the plight of cats on the Guantanamo Bay army base in Cuba. Feral cats littered the base and were routinely rounded up and euthanized. So Steve and a friend were commissioned to fly to Cuba to gather up twenty-five of the cats.

I get teary with grief and laughter when I imagine Steve cornering these savage cats on runways and under loading docks, gingerly lifting their scratching, seething bodies into carriers. I suppose that if one can see these scrawny, angry cats as creatures with a future—lives with the potential for love—then we see them as Steve saw them. I suppose we also get a sense of how God sees us.

I spent a week giving attention to birds because in the Old Testament birds tell us about God's care for the most fragile parts of creation, a sentiment reflected back on God's people.

"Who are these that fly like a cloud, and like doves to their windows?" Isaiah wonders, imagining the nations gathered up by God (Isaiah 60:8). Psalm 104:17 holds the image of cedars that provide refuge for birds: "In them the birds build their nests; the stork has its home in the fir trees."

Steve reminds me that when we see creation and all its creatures as God sees us, as beloved, we begin to see everything else differently. We, too, begin to see the world as beloved. I wonder if Jesus had the psalmist's words about sparrows in the temple in mind when he told those gathered around him to "look at the birds of the air" (Matthew 6:26).

IN THE MIDDLE AGES, Christians constructed "books of nature" called bestiaries. Christians of the time assumed that embedded in the natural world were lessons for people, that in the lives of animals we would discover lessons about who God is, that God is somehow revealed through things that creep and crawl, slide and slither.

Bestiary manuscripts compiled allegories alongside detailed illustrations. Thousands of these texts and their accompanying pictures, with beasts both real and mythical, reveal a moral or spiritual lesson. Some of the monks who created the bestiaries quickly switched from the description of the animal to the lesson discovered therein: this fish is like the Trinity, that pelican is like the sacrifice of Jesus, a rabbit displays this ethical lesson.

Cranes are one of the birds that inspire extensive theological insight. Isidore of Seville records the way cranes call out to one another when they fly, and notes that when the voice of one grows tired, another crane takes its place. Other monks, who painstakingly depicted the details of the cranes' long legs and each blue feather, were fascinated by their ability to stay awake for long stretches of time, to fly at great heights, and to hold rocks in their claws.

In one bestiary, a description of a crane becomes an opportunity to reflect on Jesus' admonitions for the disciples to "stay awake" in the gospel of Mark (13:35). Cranes watch over their brothers, protecting them from the evils of the world and warning them of the dangers of sin. The stone in their claw is Christ, the stone a true believer should carry in his mind at all times. Expert at sleeplessness, the crane reminded the monks never to drift away from their attention to God. If one does, the stone in one's claw will fall and be lost.

Other writers who observe nature in this way are carried away by the depictions of the animals themselves, often letting the allegory fall to the wayside. Pliny the Elder often gets distracted by the details. He notes that swallows gather water on their wings to wet parched earth. He describes with loving care the gentle parity of a swallow mother who equitably distributes gathered berries and insects among her chirping offspring. He records the movements of swallows with their "swift and swerving" flight. Some monks catch themselves in the diversion of these descriptions and manage to tack a pithy phrase onto the end of their reflections, some words about how God is like this or that. Other writers forget altogether, distracted by creation, distracted into tender regard.

It's this attentiveness that works itself into Psalm 84: "Even the sparrow finds a home, and the swallow a nest for herself, where she may lay her young, at your altars, O Lord of hosts, my King and my God" (Psalm 84:3). It is no surprise that sparrows and swallows made their homes in the expanses of Jerusalem's temple. These birds make their lives near people.

Swallows and sparrows thrive in the presence of human habitation, constructing their homes in cracks in walls, in deserted barns and abandoned lofts where ruins make space.

With its wide expanses of crevices and cracks, the temple was ideal for an incursion of birds. It was in this vast space of the temple where birds made their nests that God's life ran free. The temple gave shape to God's spirit, giving God's people a place to draw near to God. In Psalm 84, God welcomes swallows to pack the dirt of their nests, to line these nests with feathers, to brood patiently over a clutch of six eggs. God gives attention to the intricacies of sparrow birth. These winged creatures find room in God's holy place, building roosts in the midst of God's spirit, on the altars themselves.

The naturalist poet Mary Oliver recalls this kind of attentive regard—an opening of one's life to the intrusion of created things—in her late wife. "It has frequently been remarked about my own writings," Oliver remarks in *Our Life*, "that I emphasize the notion of attention." She observes,

> This began simply enough: to see that the way the flicker flies is greatly different from the way the swallow plays in the golden air of summer. It was my pleasure to notice such things, it was a good first step. But later, watching M. when she was taking photographs, and watching her in the darkroom, and no less watching the intensity and openness with which she dealt with friends, and strangers too, taught me what real attention is about. Attention without feeling, I began to learn, is only a report. An openness—an empathy—was necessary if the attention was to matter.[1]

Mary Oliver's words remind me of a friend who is an ornithologist. When we talk outside, I notice that every once in a while his eyes dart in the direction of a bird song. He searches the skies, seeing and hearing birds that are invisible to me. I know that he is trying to listen to me, but he's distracted—drawn away by the birds, sidetracked by something I can't see, noise that filters into the background of my world.

I imagine that God is like my neighbor. God goes about important business, yet who can't help but be diverted to look for a bird. What takes practice for me—this discipline of paying attention—is simply how God is. In God's life all creatures have weight; they cannot help but call attention. God cannot help but make protective space in God's life for them to roost and thrive.

The psalmist invites us to notice that there is a bird nesting at the altar, invites us to be drawn into the overlooked lives that carve out space in corners. As I gave my regard to birds over the course of that week, I noticed that my attention was drawn more and more to scenes in my life that I often overlook.

Most days of the week I carve out a corner in the public library to write and pray and study. I love the people here. Today this tower of books is refuge for an after-school child in a well-pressed red and blue uniform, a homeless man resting on a bench as he leafs through *Moby-Dick*, and the older adults of the mindfulness yoga class that meets in one of the empty classrooms.

Whenever I am here there are women using computers reserved for job searches, scouring for employment opportunities. On this day, a woman has brought along her two little children. The toddlers crawl under the table, around her chair, jostling for the coveted spot between their mother's feet. A few days later I notice a mother gently rocking a stroller back and forth with one hand, her little one bundled inside, napping. His mother uses her free hand to peck at the keyboard.

As I watch them all, I remember reading about a species of sparrow that builds nests with any available material. These sparrows make life out of what they can find—newspaper scraps, bits of hair, or cotton balls. Knowing these birds will ravage her sweet peas for nesting material, my sister leaves a long row of loosely tied ribbons on a wire for the sparrows to carry into the nearby garden shed.

In the library I look at these little sparrows, nesting under the computer table, and I think about other nests: the homes built for overlooked people. Tent cities and refugees in camps, shelters cropping up in the woods, the people who sleep in cars, on a friend's couch, under the doorways of church buildings—and how God can't help but pay attention to them, how they draw God's attention, how God's eyes turn toward them.

THE BIRDS OF THE TEMPLE, nesting on the altar, taught me to see with God's vision, and it was this new sight that led me to Julie. She was one of these birds, scraping together a life out of what she could find. Julie used to panhandle outside my church—or, as she would say, "fly a sign." Julie lived a fragile life, vulnerable from the beginning, a life that started out hard and never got easier. She wouldn't call herself a beggar. She didn't beg. She stood near the light at the corner of Gregson Street. Julie would walk down a stopped row of cars, and when the light changed to green she'd pace back, wait for the light to turn. I can still see the slow pace, the expectation, the resignation, the return, the beginning again.

Twenty-seven dollars. That was the magic number, the amount she needed to earn in heat or cold before quitting for the day. That would get her a room at the motel and a hit.

When addiction took control, or when times were slow and people were stingy, or when it was too cold for passersby to roll down their windows, twenty-seven dollars wasn't enough. She would sleep in a tent, look for other ways to bring in enough to get through the day, just through the day.

Julie told me how people in some of the cars that stopped would yell obscenities at her. Sometimes a driver would hold out his money and then, when Julie got close enough, grab her, put his hands on her. Others would give money, but the price was a lecture on getting her act together, not wasting her life on drugs. Most people were cold but straightforward—a dollar here, a dollar there. When I'd pull up, I'd see the steely look in her eye, bracing for whatever those cars threw out—shame or charity, usually both. She'd catch my eye, wave, relax just for a moment. The light would change.

Julie never asked much of me. I'd come out of my office at the church to bring her water when the weather got hot. I'd sit with her, sipping from a plastic bottle as she told me the gossip about our friends on the street: who was back to hustling, who was in jail. She didn't like to talk about her kids, both in foster care. I'd mention them once or twice, but that was idle talk. We might as well plan a trip to the moon. There was nothing else except getting through today.

Julie's whole life was lived on the fraying edge of mercy, a life where no one was interested in offering up much to her. One time I took Julie to get a restraining order against a man who molested her while she slept in her tent. We entered a gray, gritty office in the corner of the county jail. Double-plated glass separated us from a clerk hunched over a keyboard. He pointed us outside, to the courthouse. We walked the mile down the road, Julie's weak body staggering along.

In a room with a placard that read "Domestic Violence," a woman roughly handed us a clipboard. Julie was to document the incident. "Are you in imminent danger?" she barked.

"What?" Julie said.

"Are you in danger. Right now."

"No," Julie responded. The door slammed and Julie and I looked at each other, confused. The door opened again as the woman, without explanation, took the paperwork from our hands.

"Address of the perpetrator?" He doesn't have an address, we explained. He lives on the streets.

"There's nothing we can do for you," the woman concluded without elaboration. Protection from abuse is a privilege for those with a permanent address. Julie was out of luck. Julie was used to being out of luck. We trudged back to the church in the damp heat.

In the midst of the wreckage, Julie managed to eke out a little bit of happiness. It felt like a miracle every time. Every once in a while, she'd get a new plan, a new possibility. She'd talk excitedly about someone she'd met, or I'd hear she had taken off to South Carolina or Texas, scraped together enough money to buy a bus ticket. She'd leave and return, always ending up back on Gregson Street, back home.

Julie was stalwart in friendship. Even as life turned out to be a series of disappointments, she managed to make space within herself for others, make room in the nest of her life for whatever she could find. Somehow, she allowed herself to be surprised by kindness.

I knew that Julie's body was fragile, worn down by years of figuring out how to manage a life where her only currency was mercy. And one day, just like that, a friend found her dead in a tent. A seizure had stopped her heart. "A short, hard life," we'd say, as we looked out from the driver's seat of our passing vehicles. Another tragic life, shot through with folly. Of course, as human life is, Julie's was more complicated than that. Like all of us, she worked to string together survival and joy and more survival.

Julie never felt very comfortable coming inside the church, but she taught us to look beyond our walls, to discover where fragile birds were hiding, just out of sight. And the world was where Julie felt most at home. Our pews were sidewalks and our altar a picnic table.

So it was fitting that when Julie died, a swath of the friends she'd bound into a clutch of hope gathered on the front lawn of the church. We told stories and read from the Bible about people God loved who didn't have homes of brick and mortar. We ate sandwiches and placed Julie's ashes in the columbarium, safe now at last, and flying free in God's life.

WHEN JESUS PREACHED the Sermon on the Mount, I imagine him pausing after telling the crowd to "look at the birds of the air." He is distracted for a moment, his mind going back to the words of Psalms he heard as a child, those words bounding through him. I imagine him doing what my ornithologist neighbor does: his eye catches a flutter of movement in a tree, as a bird hops from branch to branch. I imagine Jesus' attention lingering on the birds around him, caught up where the psalmist can't help but notice: those mama swallows with their chirping babies, mouths opened wide for insects; those thick, dark nests made of muddy pebbles; those freed bodies flitting about the open air of the temple.

I meet this Jesus on a Sunday away from home, as I find my way to the local Catholic church for mass. The sanctuary is filled with little birds, children making nests within the pews and aisles. A little girl in front of me, not yet able to walk, pulls herself to standing and pats the gold cross embossed on my hymnal. Behind me a baby is laid on a quilt beside his mother; a toddler forms a mound of blankets around her on the kneeler. I can hear their laughter and sneezes echoing off the walls as the bread is held high, broken in the hands of the priest.

And so it seems like no surprise at all that I return home to discover a bird has found a way into the home I am living in for the week. It is sitting on a blue-backed chair in my living room, its white breast and its head turned towards me as I open the door. Curious, it watches me for a moment as I quietly close the curtains to darken the room. I open the front door again. It sees the light and flies into the morning.

The birds soaring through the temple, my friends Steve and Julie, the sparrows nestled in the library, birds flying across the margins of *The Saint John's Bible*—each of them has shown me that to delight in the unexpected intrusion of another is to dwell in God's life. This distraction, and God's distraction for us, has another name: love.

9

GOD OF THE VULNERABLE

*Now the Arameans on one of their raids had taken a young
girl captive from the land of Israel, and she served Naaman's
wife. She said to her mistress, "If only my lord were with the
prophet who is in Samaria! He would cure him of his leprosy."
So Naaman went in and told his lord just what the girl from
the land of Israel had said.*
—2 KING 5:2-4

This is the first day of my new life!
—HENRI NOUWEN, *THE ROAD TO DAYBREAK*

It seemed it was only a matter of time before the neighbor
boys up the street were hit by a car. Almost every day, shortly
after we pulled into the driveway, I would see the boys, nine and
eleven, leap from their porch and onto their bikes. A smooth,
long hill leads from their house at the top of the road to our
house at the bottom. But they have to cross one street to reach
our front door. It's that road that always scares me. The boys
pay attention for oncoming cars but I always hold my breath
as they near the intersection, careening through the stop sign.

One day my two-year-old and I were getting out of the car when this familiar scene played out. Arms full of toddler and grocery bags, I turned just in time to see Robby riding his bike with his brother Malcolm propped on the seat behind him. They were laughing, heads back in the wind. The distraction of joy and a misplaced tree on the corner meant that the boys couldn't see the oncoming traffic. They couldn't see the car driving down Englewood, about to cross their path. There was a screech and a loud thump as I watched the vehicle swipe the front of the bike where Robby was sitting, the white sedan smashing into his left leg.

THE OLD TESTAMENT calls our attention to fragile lives in our world. Throughout the stories of ancient Israel, we are invited to turn our attention to those overlooked and left at the margins of power. In my own world, these vulnerable lives are often those of children. I sense both the manifold dangers set before children, and also how the tenuousness of their lives stands in contrast to their resilience. My neighbor boys embody this strange amalgamation.

The Old Testament is dotted here and there with little lives. We hear about one of these lives in 2 Kings 5, in which we encounter Naaman, a wealthy, well-connected military general from the nation of Aram. He has a humiliating problem—a horrible, putrid skin disease. I imagine it looked and smelled rancid, which made it embarrassing for him to be in the company of others. This was not the expected self-presentation for any person in public life, especially not for an elite general.

In one of their recent military campaigns, Naaman's armies captured Israelites and took them as slaves. One of these slaves was a little girl. In the Hebrew, the text emphasizes how small she is—small of size and small of significance. It's a story of contrast: a nameless girl slave and a named male general. The powerless and the powerful, the "haves" and the "have nots."

The child in the story is a "little little girl"—as I would translate the Hebrew phrase—a nameless slave from a conquered people. And yet, to our surprise, one day this insignificant child speaks. She turns to Naaman's wife to suggest a possible remedy to cure her master's disease. Naaman's wife communicates these words back to her husband: "If only my lord were with the prophet who is in Samaria! He would cure him." (2 Kings 5:3). Despite the trauma of being taken to a foreign country as a slave, this child offers compassion.

After this surprisingly tender communication of a possible cure for Naaman's illness, the little little girl seems to disappear from the story. That is her one line, her one sentence bravely spoken to the mistress of the house. Her words come to us in the form of empathy. They communicate a longing, a desire for the healing of the military general who ripped her from her family, enslaved her, and brought her to a land far from her home. We are left to wonder why she responds this way, why the little little girl doesn't leave Naaman to wallow in his sores.

We find out nothing more about her story. The narrative paces along without giving us time to wonder. What happened to her family? Were they murdered in front of her? Were they, too, taken as slaves, a family torn apart by a politics outside their control? Was she afraid? Did she cry at night? Was she four or five, or eight or nine? Did she still play make-believe games in those moments between carrying pans and gathering firewood?

We are not given time to dwell on these questions. We're led on to more important things. Naaman hears of the girl's exclamation and, in his importance, goes about seeking his healing the way well-connected people do. He relies on his network of power to get him into Israel—a letter from his king to the king in Samaria. He gets payment ready: gold, silver, and expensive clothing. Naaman goes where important people go. Powerful people do powerful things, so he goes to the king of Israel, assuming that's where he'll get this miraculous healing.

Yet it isn't the king who can help Naaman. Instead, it's an easily excitable, short-tempered, bald prophet. Elisha the prophet doesn't pay much attention to the great and majestic general from Aram who stands outside his door. Instead, Elisha sends out a servant to report that Naaman's healing can be had by dunking himself in brackish water.

The instructions from the prophet for this healing are not, as he anticipated, some hocus pocus, waving of hands, chanting and rituals. Instead, Naaman is to bathe in the sewage-filled waters of the Jordan River, the place where common people bathe and defecate and feed their cattle.

We think we're being taken in one direction, only to discover the prophet turning us around and telling us to go the opposite way. We read this story standing in the shoes of Naaman. He has gone about this the way important people go about their business. Naaman does what he knows. He employs the bluster of kingly affairs, pompous parades, cash gifts, and diplomatic exchanges. And here, at the end of the narrative, he is stripped of all of this. He's reduced to a naked, scabby mess of a human being, bathing in a polluted river.

What comes out of the Jordan, what emerges, we find, is a person with the "flesh of a little child," with skin that looks like a little child (2 Kings 5:14 KJV). In Hebrew the text offers hints, helping us along, using the same word to describe both the reborn Naaman and the little little girl who initiates this healing story. Naaman's skin is like her skin. His body is like her body. All this time, God was turning the story back to the one Naaman passed over, the one we disregarded: a nameless slave child, a very little girl.

The ancient rabbis have a saying: "We do not see things as they are. We see things as we are."[1] Naaman sees importance in political connections and wealth. And he learns that the God of Israel is the God to whom all are precious. God sees as God is.

I wonder if Naaman, standing naked on the riverbank, wiping away the stinking mud and swatting at biting flies—I wonder if he realizes that God loves him. I wonder if he finds that his life means something to God, that God loves him without any additional fanfare. I wonder if, stripped of wealth and power, Naaman comes to know that, in God, his life means as much as that of a little little slave girl. Which is to say his life means everything.

THE DAY AFTER my neighbor boys are hit by a car, the street outside my house is quiet. The ambulance and fire engine are gone. There's no trace of the crash that happened the day before. But my body still pulses with the energy, still hears the cry, still remembers dropping everything to run. On instinct, I had dropped what I had in the street outside my car—my bag, my groceries, even my two-year-old. I turned and I ran toward Robby.

After the sound of metal and tires, one of my neighbors carried Robby back to his house, his leg drenched in blood.

I rushed back, grabbed my daughter, and sprinted up the hill to their front porch, where I held the boy's newborn sister as Robby's mother cradled her son, the ambulances wailing in the distance. Soon enough an EMT would pronounce that the severe gash on his leg would heal. An hour later, my hands would shake as I gathered up my scattered groceries from the street, pushing from my mind what could have taken place if the boys had been at the intersection only a second earlier.

On that porch, my arms around my neighbor's baby girl, I remembered that God is like that, too, leaving everything behind to run after us, leaving her own child in the street, rushing toward us. God does not see things as they are. God see things as God is. God sees the inverse of privilege. What we learn from Naaman is that wealth and standing obscure belovedness. And when God sees us—when God sees the smallness of our lives, when God sees each of us stripped of everything, with nothing left—God sees a beloved. God is leaving everything behind and running toward us.

ONE MORNING I ask our own little little ones at church to go outside during Sunday school to collect things they think are precious. They clutch these treasures and process in with them during the opening hymn, anointing our worship table with leaves and rocks, a dead worm, and a rusty toy car retrieved from a ditch.

Naaman would likely look askance at deceased invertebrates gracing the table of our Lord. It is Naaman who balks at Elisha's suggestion that his healing will come from bathing in the waters of the Jordan. "I thought that for me he would surely come out, and stand and call on the name of the Lord his God, and would wave his hand over the spot, and cure the leprosy!" he pouts (2 Kings 5:11). Even so, there are cleaner rivers than the Jordan in which to bathe.

It's ridiculous, this whole business. "He turned and went away in a rage" (5:12). The problem for Naaman is not the difficulty of the task but the absurdity of it. The social order Naaman expects, oriented towards respect and wealth, towards the exception-taking that defines Naaman's existence—this world has passed away. What's left is a stagnant ditch of rotting garbage.

In the third century, the theologian Tertullian responded to similar objections from a group of Christians called Docetists. These Docetists were scandalized by the claim that God could take on the fullness of frail and ragged humanity in the person of Jesus Christ, complete with bowel movements, skinned knees, and hay fever. Human flesh was, by definition, that which was not divine. Jesus, the Docetists surmised, must have been the great imitator, taking on the likeness of humanity, not true skin and veins and bone. God was other than the messiness of created things.

But for Tertullian, God entering into the world in a body with knees that ached and a craving for salty foods was enough of a reason to believe. "I am becoming a fool in the world through believing the foolish things of God," he declared in *On the Flesh of Christ*. "The Son of God was crucified: there is no shame, because it is shameful. And the Son of God died: it is by all means to be believed, because it is absurd. And, buried, He rose again: it is certain, because impossible."[2]

THERE IS A LINE of houses in the southeast end of Portland, Oregon, where a strange experiment is taking place. It's a testimony to the kind of absurdity Tertullian found credible.

A sort of holy foolishness is unfolding there in the L'Arche community. Whenever I would pull into the driveway to visit my friends there, I wondered what I would find inside: Erin listening to her Beach Boys albums, Ben and Marilyn making dinner, perhaps Joni leafing through old picture books, searching for photos of her mother.

The L'Arche community is a place where people with and without intellectual disabilities share life together. In my early twenties I lived in one of these homes, an outpost of hope rooted in an ordinary-looking neighborhood. In this community the assistants and the core members (the people with disabilities who make up the center of our lives) carry on the absurd work of giving and receiving gifts.

L'Arche began with a call from God. A Catholic layperson named Jean Vanier first considered the powerful possibilities of corporate daily life in the late 1940s in Harlem, where he learned of Friendship House, a community of shared life for black and white people. Vanier went on to observe the radical experiments of communal living that were taking place with Dorothy Day and the Catholic Worker movement.

As Vanier grew in faith and experienced more of what these intentional communities offered, he sensed God calling him to the poor. A Catholic priest helped Vanier find his way to an institution for the disabled called Val Fleury in the small village of Trostly, France. In the 1960s, people with disabilities lived in institutions like Val Fleury, which reeked of isolation and poverty. "It was both an attraction and a repulsion," Vanier recalled as he met the people who lived in the gray, concrete building—"an attraction towards a mystery, and a repulsion in the face of abnormality."[3] Vanier left to teach philosophy in Canada, but something inside him had been transformed by his encounters with people who had been cast aside and hidden away.

In 1964, when Vanier returned to France, L'Arche came to life. He wrote about the community in early journals: "On the edge of the forest of Compiègne, L'Arche has opened its first home for the mentally and physically handicapped. These family-like homes, each welcoming from four to nine boys, at least twenty years old, are lifelong homes. They are the first of a group of homes which will be linked together with work-shops, a cultural centre, a chapel and the necessary medical help."[4]

In the beginning, Vanier lived in a home with two men, Raphael Semi and Philippe Seux. They had no indoor plumb-ing, and reports are that the cooking was awful. But they called it L'Arche, "the ark," a place of safety in a drowning world. Others came to live alongside them. The community grew.

In early black-and-white films from those first days in L'Arche, young men are gathered together, singing folk songs in French and picking apples. In another shot they bend over desks, painting on white canvases with the help of volunteers. "The important thing is to know that someone loves you," a youthful Vanier says exuberantly to the camera.

I first heard about L'Arche from my seminary professors. They told me it was a community where people with intellec-tual differences come to know that God loves them, that they are needed, and that all people are the same in our longing for friendship and community. I'd also heard that L'Arche could teach my heart some things—lessons about peace and hope, about being a sign of God's love in the world, about gentleness.

The people in Portland's L'Arche community had said they'd like to welcome me but first I'd need to stay the weekend in a community near my home on the East Coast. They wanted me to try it out, to make sure it was a good fit. The closest L'Arche home to me was in Washington, D.C., so one warm afternoon in mid-summer I hopped on the Metro and made my way to the Adams Morgan neighborhood in the heart of Washington, D.C.

It hit me all at once as I turned right onto Euclid Avenue: I knew nothing about people with intellectual disabilities. My life had been sheltered from such people, sheltered in school, in the suburbs, by a culture that keeps people with disabilities out of the way of people like me. I didn't know what to expect, and I was afraid.

Those first steps up to Euclid House led me into a new life. I learned much over the next three and a half years at L'Arche, but the most important lesson was to always be ready for the surprise of another person's life. Living among my friends in L'Arche meant discovering God at work unexpectedly. I learned to pay attention to "little little" lives within a global history written for those with power, money, and influence. I soon discovered that flourishing in this community meant giving up expectations of others, of what people could and couldn't do, of the ways we communicate or pray or sing, and of what it means to be human.

But living in L'Arche also meant releasing the expectations I had for myself. Until I lived in L'Arche, I didn't realize how accustomed I'd become to a narrative of excellence and predictable progression. I'd been trained my whole life to work at perfecting myself. I expected a slow pattern of self-improvement for myself and others. In L'Arche I came to discover that I was packed with expectations of who I should be, what was good, and what was expected.

The L'Arche community invites people to put all that aside. That's one of its gifts, and one of the gifts of people with lives immunized against predictable progress. These beloved people defy perfectibility. The core members' bodies, their minds, their lives are resistant to ableist expectations. We simply receive one another as we are: in this moment, in this space, around this table, on this walk, as we sing this hymn or wash each other's feet. We receive the gift of each other's lives, all that is available now.

The community creates slow rhythms designed to surprise us at the possibility of human flourishing. How could any group of people take so long to prepare dinner each night? How was it possible that these housemates could care so much that everyone was able to participate in the preparation of the meal, that everyone's hands were stirring, chopping, or simmering the food before us? How could it be that there was always enough, that our food stretched to the stray neighbor or church member or that guy you just met up the block? How was it that so many people could gather around that rickety dinner table?

Jean Vanier writes that many of us "live with the burden of unconscious guilt."[5] We feel we are not who we should be. So it is a wonder, a profound surprise, to hear you are simply enough as you are. It is a wonder to be told you don't need to defend yourself, don't have to get any better or smarter or be able to put on your shoes by yourself to be worthy of the attention of another. It is a wonder to hear that the gifts you have are all you need. It is a wonder to discover the gift of your life giving off warmth to others. It is a wonder to be told you are no bother at all and that everything happening around you says, "I love you."

"To love people is to recognize their gifts and help these unfold," writes Vanier. "It is also to accept their wounds and be patient and compassionate toward them."[6] The mission of L'Arche is to be attentive to all of it: the wounds and the gifts, the insecurities and the pain and the hope.

A DECADE LATER, living far from my friends in Portland, here on the other side of the country I find I am in the midst of this holy work once again. Friends from other L'Arche communities have joined together here in Durham to bring a sign of hope into the neighborhood. We wait and hope, pray and dream for a beloved community, a place where people with and without disabilities share life and faith together. When I'm in doubt, when the paperwork of residential group homes and Medicaid waivers feels unbearable and dehumanizing, I find myself turning back to the God of the vulnerable. I know God is for us, for L'Arche, because this God took Naaman, a great Aramite general, and gave him a body like that of a little slave girl.

On these days when it seems like our community will always be a dream, I remember my first walk toward L'Arche in Washington, D.C. I think about climbing the steps of the brownstone that led to my first L'Arche home. I remember that mingled in with my fear and misgiving, I was waiting to be surprised.

We're in good company. We worship a God of surprises, a God who turns political and religious structures upside down through the lives of the weakest and the most vulnerable in our world. This God is in the habit of finding a way back to children and women and shepherds and "sinners," condemning the righteous teachers who think they've got the law figured out. This God weaves grace and hope into the lives of Gentiles and eunuchs, widows and tax collectors. This God places their lives at the center of the story of God's presence on earth. We find that when we are among the "little little" lives of this world, we are in God's presence.

God of the Table

The LORD appeared to Abraham by the oaks of Mamre, as he sat at the entrance of his tent in the heat of the day. He looked up and saw three men standing near him. When he saw them, he ran from the tent entrance to meet them, and bowed down to the ground.
    —GENESIS 18:1-2

It turns out that there are lots of things you cannot explain except by telling stories, which do not explain or define or account for them hardly at all, but do give you a subtle and telling sense of what we mean when we use the words holy *and* miracle *and* God.
    —BRIAN DOYLE, "ALL IN ONE"

While it's easy to notice others in our world as God notices them—images of God in birds and children—it's hard to talk about God. But once a year, on Trinity Sunday, the church has the tradition of spending a Sunday attempting to get our minds around a God who is Father, Son, and Holy Spirit. Of course, we have an impossible task in sorting out a God who is both three and one at the same time. But on Trinity Sunday we keep trying.

There are endless ways to get the Trinity wrong, because every time we start talking about God—every time we try to consolidate the mystery down to a metaphor—we end up falling into one heresy or another: modalism, adoptionism, Arianism, Sabellianism. The heresies of the church fall onto one side or another, either emphasizing the oneness of God at the expense of three distinct persons, or creating a hierarchy out of God, elevating one person of the Trinity over the others.

I tend to avoid the language of heresy. Anabaptists have been called heretics since we broke away from the magisterial Reformation in the sixteenth century, leaving me unsure that this theological distinction is helpful. I've also seen through-out Christian history how the word *heretic* is used to scare us away from one another, to designate who is in and who is out, and to curtail engagement and conversation.

But in his writings, the British theologian Rowan Williams taught me to appreciate what the church intended to say when it condemned heresy. Denouncing heretics wasn't only about keeping out opinions the church didn't like, though it was certainly that. Heresy, Williams helped me see, also did the important work of naming the doctrines that cleared up mystery too quickly—theological positions that put too fine a point on descriptions of God.

The concept of heresy helps us to understand the problem with saying that the Trinity is like candy corn or a clover or an apple. These attempts at metaphor are too easy and too neat. Heresy cuts away the knots, replacing them with the appearance of order. Heresies turn God into an idea we can manipulate with our good deeds or our intellect or our power.

But God is stranger and wilder than that. As Isaiah reminds us, if we understand something, it is not God (Isaiah 55:8-9).

Behind all this piling up of heresies around the Trinity lies the fact that we're people who easily fall into idolatry. We like to have a god we can wrap our minds around. We like a god we can control, a god we can move from place to place, an idol we can pick up and place on our side. Human history is riddled with attempts to manage a god who does what we want, when we want, no questions asked. Heresies, as the church has often named them, remind us not to get too comfortable with the gods of our own making.

One way the Russian Orthodox Church tries to avoid making God into our own image through idolatry is by prohibiting icons that picture God the Father. God has no body, after all, and to offer up a physical image of God will consistently miss the mark. The exception to this rule is the icon of the visitation of the three angels to Sarah and Abraham at Mamre in Genesis 18.

In this story, Abraham and Sarah are going about their business when three visitors show up at their tent in the heat of the day. Something stirs within Abraham. He is delighted and awed by the encounter, and he bows low before running about in a frenzy. Most of the story is spent telling us about the detailed preparation for the shared meal, and almost no time is given to the depiction of the three visitors. There is foot washing, hurried baking—butter, milk, and a calf "tender and good" (Genesis 18:7). Abraham watches as his visitors savor the feast. It is then that the good news erupts. Sarah, elderly and barren, will have a son.

In the Orthodox tradition this story holds an image of the Trinity. God appears quickly, without fanfare, in a flash.

Three-who-are-one delight in the sharing of human life. And then the strangers disappear again. They're off, silently into the night, the sound of Sarah's laughter still in the air.

There's something strange and wonderful in this story. Here in the Old Testament, the Trinity shows up for lunch. God is made known in the everydayness of Sarah and Abraham's life, revealed at the dinner table. God's story can't be told without their story. God's identity is woven into their bodies and their futures.

I keep a wood-mounted copy of Andrei Rublev's icon of this story in my study. Three people sit in chairs around a table, similar in their faces yet not identical. Conspicuous wings sprout from their backs, and a halo rings each head. I keep this icon in sight to remind me that God makes appearances in human lives, that God finds and surprises us, like a guest and like a friend, often when we least expect it. When I look at Rublev's icon I wonder if the best way for us to have something to say about the mystery of the Trinity is to look for God revealed in stories like the table at Mamre. Stories invite us in, to get a feel for something without pinning it down. Good stories are humble in their claims about truth. Stories are about forming our imagination, the fleeting, rushing moment of revelation before it gets away again.

I love the story of the appearance of the three to Abraham and Sarah. Abraham, resigned to his infertility by Sarah, intends to find another way around the problem of absent progeny. And instead he finds himself unexpectedly caught up in an encounter with God. There's no lead-up, no foreshadowing. Unlike the other attempts of Abraham to cast his genetic line into the future, God's promise requires no plotting, no bamboozling, no intrigue.

It is disarming in its ordinariness. Abraham looks up, we read in Genesis, and sees three visitors. But while we are told by the writer of this story that it is actually God showing up, Abraham is not privy to our insights, as readers of the text. He simply observes three guests who appear at the camp. Abraham winds his life into their life. He greets them, running to bring these strangers what he has. God welcomes this—the hospitality of the shared meal. God, the three in one, whole and without need—this God receives what Abraham and Sarah have to offer. God takes the gifts of meat and milk.

But there is more surprise here, more richness. The strangers announce with certainty that Sarah will have a baby. Sarah, in her old age, will bear a son. Abundance is met with abundance. Is anything too wonderful for God?

In Rublev's icon the three persons of the Godhead sit around Sarah and Abraham's table. The persons at the center and right turn toward the third: God the Father. A tree behind the middle person reveals that this person is Christ, the root of Jesse. On the right is the Holy Spirit, making a gesture with one hand. I have imagined that in the third person the Spirit is inviting us to the table, welcoming us to sit and eat beside God, to take of the abundant surprise, the laughter-inducing surprise of God's overflowing love. The third person of Rublev's icon reminds us that it is the work of the Spirit to make space for us in God's life.

AS I'VE TRIED to talk about God, which I do almost every Sunday from the pulpit, I'm grateful to discover the grace in speaking the unspeakable, a grace in learning to fail, a grace in finding new ways to talk about a God who is always appearing in and out of view. We may find ourselves searching for a new story that gives us a moment of revelation. I suspect the same is true for storytellers who can pick up a mystery for a moment, then let it go again.

Perhaps this is why the Old Testament is the best steward for our discovery of the Trinity. It is in this part of the Bible where we find the Trinity in three companions eating around Sarah and Abraham's table. And it is here that God, three in one, is on display in the creation of the world. Every third year, the Revised Common Lectionary reserves Genesis 1 for Trinity Sunday because of the verses spoken by God for the creation of human beings: "Then God said, 'Let us make humankind in our image, according to our likeness'" (Genesis 1:26).

As the early mothers and fathers of the church were searching around for stories that gave words to God as Father, Son, and Holy Spirit, they lifted up this account of creation at the beginning of the biblical story. Theologians like John Chrysostom and Gregory of Nyssa heard in this story inklings of the Trinity. God proclaims, "Let us make people in our image." God speaks in the plural—as an "us," a community, the one God proclaimed as active in the Holy Spirit brooding above the waters. A creative love born out of an ever-intertwining oneness.

If we are to find God, we will do so in a story. And here at creation we have a story about a colossal bursting forth of every good and perfect thing, an eruption of gifts of pomegranate seeds and tigers and waterfalls, of shooting stars burning across a total emptiness. God fills it up with things that bray and howl and grow and creep. These stories let us glimpse God, the holy mystery of a God who is three yet one, a relation of ever-producing love who bends down to the ground and laughs in delight as a caterpillar crawls over her fingers.

What we discover is that God isn't a part of the created world. Instead, God loves, creates, delights, and roams. In other creation stories written around the time of the Genesis story, the gods are pieces of the created order. They take the form of creatures and tides. And these gods are fickle. The Ancient Near Eastern gods are often cruel, inflicting pain and death through wind and fire, storm and rock. They demand sacrifices. The gods bicker and war with one another, while human life becomes the collateral damage of their infighting.

In Genesis, something else happens. God sets down human beings as a seal, an emblem of love. People become the image of God's love, others revealing this love because love requires others. Our lives happen inside of this love, inside of a God who is love within God's self, where creation echoes back that life is a response to being loved. The world is a gift, you are a gift, we are gifts to one another. It's the story we tell to each other, this creation story, to say: "You were put here in love, to love because you are God's beloved." What we have is a story where God slips into view and out again, known and unknown.

When Gregory Nazianzus thought about the Trinity, he knew this slippage. For Gregory these were lights going in and out of view. He writes,

> No sooner do I conceive of the one than I am illumined by the splendor of the three; no sooner do I distinguish them than I am carried back to the one. When I think of anyone of the three I think of him as the whole, and my eyes are filled, and the greater part of what I am thinking escapes me. I cannot grasp the greatness of that one so as to attribute a greater greatness to the rest. When I contemplate the three together, I see but one torch, and cannot divide or measure out the undivided light.[1]

"I cannot grasp the greatness," wrote Gregory. *I cannot grasp it*. God slips past as we try again, get a glimpse and then wait for another moment. We tell the story in wonder. We see it, observe it—one in three; three in one.

I AM ON THE LOOKOUT for stories to help me pick up the mystery of the Trinity. The Old Testament's stories of the Trinity also taught me to look closer at the world around me, and like Sarah and Abraham, to discover the three in one hiding there in plain sight.

A couple years ago my friend Ann started to feel pain in her foot. It wasn't uncommon. A car accident years ago resulted in injuries that left Ann open to a variety of debilitating infections. But this time, when the pain continued and began to climb up her leg, she knew it was time to go to the emergency room. It was there she got the news. This time the infection couldn't be cured. The surgeon would need to amputate her leg, just below the knee. Ann was frightened. We were all frightened. There was barely time to grieve before the surgery.

Ann is a woman of great faith whom I met at the church I once served. One way she deepens that faith is by coming to church each morning for prayer. Cullen, my friend and colleague, started this practice of early prayer, as he opened the door to our downtown church each weekday morning at 7:30 a.m. A little band gathers in the sanctuary to pray. A woman from the office building across the street stops by most mornings. A few of the men who call our church property home and ask for money on the corner drop in for weak coffee and strong psalms. We always get a few strangers who have seen the welcome sign from their car windows or as they waited for the bus on the corner.

But Alberto comes almost every morning. We met him last year when he came to the church, looking to see if we had work for him. Alberto's only language is Spanish, so most of us get by conversing with him using our limited high school language skills. Alberto is patient with us.

Sometimes the numbers are small at morning prayer: just Alberto, Ann, and Cullen, a little trinity in themselves, hands held together as they close in the Lord's Prayer—Alberto in Spanish, and Ann and Cullen in English.

When Alberto comes to pray one morning, he learns from Cullen of Ann's amputation and extended hospital stay, which was the only reason for her absence from morning prayer. He is frantic. "Hospital," he tells Cullen. "*Hoy.*" Today we're going to the hospital. We have to see her. Cullen does his best to communicate bus routes and room numbers, not quite sure the information he is giving is accurate or communicated well in his broken Spanglish.

Cullen shows up at the hospital later that afternoon, hurrying from a meeting. He rushes toward the hospital elevator. He doesn't expect that Alberto will have the time or energy to navigate an hour of buses or the vast Duke University Hospital system. As Cullen pushes the button for the sixth floor, as the doors are about to close, a hand reaches in and stops them. The doors widen again, and there stands Alberto. "*Muy rápido,*" he scolds Cullen, as they ride the elevator to Ann's room.

A few minutes later, the three of them sit together, Cullen and Alberto forming a circle with Ann in the hospital bed where she lies. As Ann shares her insights into theologies of pain and disability, Alberto nods gently, affirming the sound of Ann's voice. They stay for an hour. Alberto brings Ann a

Bible. Toward the end they take hands, as they have so many mornings before, and they pray the prayer Jesus taught us, in Spanish and in English.

And God is like this, too. One body but different, speaking a common language of prayer but in different tongues. God is like this, bearing gifts in God's self, gifts of presence and prayer. God is there, three strangers who speak remarkable news. God is a body that is broken but whole, a body made of vulnerable parts and honored parts, bearing scars, all bearing together. God is like this, always returning to love, always returning us to a community of love, a being that cannot be without one another, a shared life bound up in love.

COMMUNION IS THE STORY of God's interdwelling life that the church tells to one another around a table. Partaking of communion together, we remember the Passover meal Jesus celebrated around the table with his disciples. Yet I cannot help but think of this shared meal also as a reenactment of the time that the Trinity materialized as guests around Sarah and Abraham's table.

I suspect that my love of Sarah and Abraham's feast is why I take such delight in the preparation of the monthly communion meal for my church. When the weather is cool enough for our little house to stand the 450-degree heat emanating from our rickety oven, I bake the communion bread we will break on Sunday. It's an important part of the ritual for me, a reminder that the table we set on Sunday will begin here in my labor, that it begins with ground wheat and crushed grapes.

As I measure the flour and water, mixing in the warmed yeast, I remember the words of Menno Simons:

> Just as natural bread is made of many grains, pulverized by
> the mill, kneaded with water, and baked by the heat of the
> fire, so is the church of Christ made up of true believers,
> broken in their hearts with the mill of the divine Word,
> baptized with the water of the Holy Ghost, and with the
> fire of pure, unfeigned love made into one body.[2]

Sometimes I knead the dough in long, smooth strokes, working it until I can hold it up to the light, pulling it thin between my fingers, a test that tells me the gluten is ready. Other weeks I cover a glutenous mixture in a large, green bowl before placing it in the sun. The dough rises over a couple days without any help from me, without my work.

Some months at church we come forward to receive the bread, but at other times we gather in a circle, offering a torn piece to our neighbor, the bread passed from hand to hand around our wide arc. Our table is at the center, and we gather around it, a body in motion as those around the circle come and go, as we come to find others have joined us, a life familiar and at the same time strange, unknowable.

On each communion Sunday, a steady hand helps guide Wallace to the place where I stand, tearing pieces of the bread. Wallace was born blind and is now crippled by old age. Over the years it has been harder for him to navigate the physical world. On occasion I go to see him in the one-bedroom home he manages with stealth and efficiency, but it is harder for him to make his way to church. Wallace often reminds me that, although he feels too unsteady to walk down the street to the building where we meet, not wishing to chance the ruts and roots, he is still a member. He tithes regularly, keeps up correspondence on his computer, and listens to every Sunday sermon. Often he'll call to talk over some of my more outlandish theological points. One day Wallace called to say he wanted to be sure he came to church once a month. He wanted to be with us on communion Sundays. Everything else in our worship he can access on the Internet: the service and songs, the announcements and updates. But he could not receive the bread and cup without other people. It wouldn't mean anything at all without a gathered body, without all of us there together. He needed the holy place of God's body coming down on the communion table. As we gather on these Sundays, I am called back to the table of Sarah and Abraham. The God revealed to them sits at a banquet, one freely given, a gift without strings attached, set not only for nourishment but for pleasure, for the joy of company, the gift of friendship, the work of their hands now for the shared life of God. But here, in this story, Abraham and Sarah don't yet join the three. Sarah remains by the cooking fire. Abraham watches as the visitors eat. It will only be in the New Testament where Jesus, God's body in flesh, finally includes his disciples at the Passover table, a meal for each of us.

The body of God, sharing the meal, the invitation to inhabit God's life—we don't get this from metaphors or from charts and graphs. We know God through stories, in the times when we are drawn into the love of the Father, Son, and Holy Spirit. We know God when we are drawn into the lives of others, when we are surprised by the life of another, surprised by God's abundance, surprised to see our lives reflected back in a community bound to God, woven into one another. We know God when we glimpse, however fleeting, pictures of the world as it ought to be.

This is why heresies of assuredness are destructive and have been devastating to the church over the course of our history.

God is mysterious, ever opening us to new possibilities, new surprises, new laughter. And we will discover along the way that people are like that, too. God is a relationship of constant unveiling, just as we are always doing the work of opening ourselves up to friendship, to being surprised by the stranger who finds her way to our door, the stranger who has news for us we could not imagine.

The Trinity reminds us to resist the urge to clear up the mystery of one another. When we do, we're committing our own heresy of certainty, certain that this person is too different, too strange, for me to draw near to her round the table. The Trinity sets the table to welcome us into the strangeness of one another. Here we discover a way to allow the other to be strange without possession, without having to make them ours.

11

God of Friendship

So Naomi returned together with Ruth the Moabite, her daughter-in-law, who came back with her from the country of Moab. They came to Bethlehem at the beginning of the barley harvest.
—RUTH 1:22

Without community there is no liberation, only the most vulnerable and temporary armistice between an individual and her oppression.
—AUDRE LORDE

The Old Testament gives us stories of God's life touching down to earth, and we call these moments holy. The Scriptures also hold within them stories of holiness elongated into a sustained encounter with another. We call that friendship.

The story of Naomi and Ruth tells us how women's friendship is sustenance through times of adversity and peril. This is a chronicle of survival and difference. At the beginning of the book of Ruth, two paths form along a common intimacy of tragedy. Ruth's story centers on two choices. One is a return to

biological family—to stability and familiarity. The other is the
creation of home outside of the bonds of kinship. This second
story is one of friendship.

The husbands of Ruth, Naomi, and Naomi's other daughter-
in-law, Orpah, are picked off by disease, one by one. The book
of Ruth spares no feeling on the death of Ruth and Naomi's
family. First Naomi's husband dies; then, like vapor, the children are dead. The unimaginable takes place in two verses.
The two sons die. In a matter-of-fact way, the Hebrew reports,
"the two of them, both." Gone.

With her daughters-in-law left to fend for themselves as
vulnerable widows, Naomi entreats them to return to their
homes, to their mothers, and to new marriages. Orpah returns
to the Moabites, presumably to the boundaries of married life,
repeating the pattern of marriage as self-protection. The rabbis explain that this is how Orpah gets her name, a derivative
of the verb "to return."

By contrast, Ruth refuses to leave Naomi. She clings. She
clings, we read, in the same way that Adam and Eve cling to
one another, the phrase lifted up from Genesis where we read
that a man leaves his mother and father, and clings now to
his wife. Ruth pleads with her mother-in-law after being told
twice to return to the Moabites, her people of origin:

> Do not press me to leave you
>   or to turn back from following you!
> Where you go, I will go;
>   where you lodge, I will lodge;
> your people shall be my people,
>   and your God my God.
> Where you die, I will die—
>   there will I be buried.

> May the Lord do thus and so to me,
>   and more as well,
> if even death parts me from you! (Ruth 1:16-17)

Some of us have heard these verses read at weddings. They are a type of vow, like the promises between partners in a marriage. Yet these are words of friendship, between two women binding their lives together—words that name the condition of lives already bound together by grief and longing. They are also words that mark instability, the homes made by refugees, by beggars, foreigners, and victims. They are words spoken by the bearer of a crushed life, women holding on to one another, where friendship is survival.

Because of this, Ruth is a story that complicates our sense of being at home. It is a story that confounds where home happens and between whom, where intimacy happens, within what boundaries, and how those boundaries are blurred between peoples and borders and families. The author sets Orpah over against Ruth. Orpah is the one who chooses the stable world of biological family; Ruth chooses outside kinship by binding herself to Naomi, her companion and friend.

This commitment to extending the boundaries of belonging reaches back to Ruth from the New Testament, where Jesus shows little interest in biological family. In the New Testament Jesus tells an astonished crowd that his mother and brothers are those who do the will of God, not those who share his biology or household of origin. Whoever leaves mother, father, brother, or sister for Jesus' sake will receive a reward. Jesus will divide houses, rip apart husbands and wives, mothers and daughters (Matthew 19:29).

As I hear the words of Jesus, I cannot forget that Ruth's story is one of death. It is about death along the way, about the death that happens when grief gives way for the space of another, when we clear out the closet of our life and let someone move in. I remember this when I hear her vow to Naomi, not as triumphant, but as aching.

Reading Ruth in this way changes the way I hear Jesus' call to disassociate from family. What if instead of rejection, we are meant to hear a call to the expansiveness of friendship: opening up our lives to others, some of whom we may not have expected, being surprised by friendships that find their way to us? What if friendship opens up a different kind of fertility, one that is nonprocreative, one that yields only flowers that never turn to fruit—beauty without production, without possession?

For this reason, more than any other story in the Bible, the friendship of Ruth and Naomi is the cipher through which I understand the church, what Peter Dula describes as a *fugitive ecclesia*. As the church we are offered an elusive interconnectedness as an earthly body of Christ, not a constant and fixed institution. The church is rare, writes Dula, found "in the occasional intimacy of two or three."[1] Ruth and Naomi remind us, as does Jesus, that the space where God's life occurs isn't necessarily in church programs or Sunday school classes but in companionship, a spark of God's life—unexpected, unplanned, and uncalculated.

Church is often trust in that which I cannot control, the shared life of another without institutionally mandated promises or production. The book of Ruth invites us to consider an ecclesiology of occasion, the church as boundedness to another. We grapple with the fragility of what is possible, that we will come in and out of each other's lives, that we will find ourselves failing at overcoming our otherness and, perhaps, trying again. Along the way we may come to discover that this love grows and extends outward beyond our biological kinship, into a beloved who is strange and similar, all at the same time.

DESPITE THE POWER of this story, the Old Testament is an unlikely place to look for those who want to understand the kinship of friends. Friendship is understated in the Old Testament, inattention rooted in Israel's composition as a people whose identity is passed on from one generation to the next through progeny. Biological kin is the plumb line of the Old Testament. It begins with Abraham, called out from all the peoples of the earth. "I will indeed bless you, and I will make your offspring as numerous as the stars of heaven and as the sand that is on the seashore," God tells "the father of many nations" in Genesis 22.

Friendship is the foil of procreation. It is nonproductive, making nothing but pleasure and joy for the friends who share in it. There are no rituals to secure permanent ties of friendship, no economy gained from it. No land is passed on, no descendants indebted to the relationship, no one whose responsibility it would be to remember the union, no future. Instead, friendship is an end in itself, as one's friend is reflected back in the other, mirrors of human possibility and frailty.

Only a handful of Israelites in the Old Testament are said to have friends. These stories of friendship mark the tensions around ethnic reproduction that is central to Israel's early identity.[2] One of the few friendships discussed in the Old Testament is found in Genesis, placed in the epic tale of Joseph and his brothers. It is a cautionary tale about friendship, a warning about choosing the self-centered love of friendship over family. The story of these friends, Judah and Hirah, sounds an alarm about friendship, cautioning us away from the distracting loyalties created by friends.

In Genesis, the brother who emerges into prominence next to Joseph is Judah, the eldest. The Bible is a book with a solid plotline of reversals of fortune for eldest brothers, so it's not surprising that in this story we discover that Judah has fallen on hard times. Judah orchestrated the sale of his own brother Joseph into slavery, eliminating his father's beloved child as a potential rival. We can imagine it is the haunting terror of his father's loss that leads Judah away from his family of origin to settle in a foreign land.

And in the ensuing years Judah makes a friend.

Over time, living alongside this friend, Hirah, Judah watches his children killed, one by one. One child dies mysteriously; the other fails to give justice to a Canaanite wife named Tamar, rejecting her right to pass on the ethnic line of Judah's family. The price for Onan's betrayal is his life.

Judah's first son marries Tamar but dies mysteriously, "wicked in the sight of the Lord" (Genesis 38:7). His second son then marries Tamar, in the custom of marriage in which a man marries his brother's widow, but refuses to procreate with her. He, too, dies. After the first two sons die, followed shortly by his wife, the heartbroken Judah becomes intent on protecting his last remaining son from what he can only assume is Tamar's bad luck. He tells the widowed woman that she must return to her home of origin and wait until his youngest son has grown old enough to marry her.

This cultural practice of levirate marriage ensured justice to widows. Without a guarantee of a husband, widows—especially older widows—would be expendable, cast aside for more procreatively promising young women. With no protection, this was the only possibility for women whose futures were tied to their husbands or male relatives. Passing on of genetic rites from one son to the next guaranteed justice for women in ancient Israel.

But Judah does not arrange a marriage between his youngest son and Tamar. He flees once more, back to his friend, Hirah, the Adullamite. Hirah is the escape from justice for Tamar. In going to Hirah, Judah flees the responsibility of marrying his son to his potentially lethal daughter-in-law. In Genesis, friendship is cast as a form of selfishness, where "friendship and marriage-and-family," writes Leon Kass, "are mutually exclusive alternatives."[3]

I AM NOT PARTICULARLY GOOD at friendship. I am mostly a recipient of an unmerited gift, which is the story of my existence and the summation of my faith. My friends are often chasing after me through my stony silences, the seasons when my own self-pity makes it difficult to do much relating well, the times when I am knee deep in my own metaphorical pile of unwashed dishes. And still, Gwyneth sends me a card and pictures of her round-cheeked babies. Still, zwieback appears in bags under my chair at church. Still, Isaac faithfully reschedules coffee or a phone call.

I am grateful for these friendships and how they show me something that lies beyond my narrow horizon. These are the friendships that have been most central to my life. If kinship, the relations of families knit together by biology, are primarily those constructed in similitude, friendship offers another practice. Paul Waddell writes that friendship "repositions us by pulling us out of ourselves, by pulling us beyond the confines of our narrow world into that vastly different world of the other."[4]

The temporary flaring up of the church in the form of friendship is powerful and transformative. We are able to see beyond our own horizon, in the midst of the complexity of differences and boundaries. Audre Lorde and Adrienne Rich have echoed back the story of Ruth and Naomi as a cipher for friendships as survival strategy. I've needed stories like this, signposts of friendship, to help me understand the difficult work of friendship across boundaries of ethnicity, race, and class. Their story is an echo of the cross-ethnic friendship of Naomi and Ruth.

We are given a rare window into the friendship of Lorde and Rich in a three-hour interview recorded on August 30, 1979. The edited results of their conversation appear in what is now a foundational text of womanist theory: Lorde's compiled essays, *Sister Outsider*. In the portion preserved in writing, Rich asks the questions, calling out Lorde's story, giving her the template to allow her theories to emerge. It is a friendship of making space for another to come into view, sometimes in robust and beautiful ways and at other times in pain and conflict. [5]

The conversation starts with a cool, theoretical tone. It's academic, the kind of interview a journalist could adequately perform. But as they discuss their teaching experiences and their shared inadequacy, something shifts. Lorde explains how "there are different choices facing Black and white women in life, certain specifically different pitfalls surrounding us because of our experience, our color." Rich knows this has something to do with her, that their racialized difference means something for their friendship.

There's a tenderness and pain to the exchange that follows. To read the conversation is to listen in on intimacy. Lorde explains that her journals are replete with snippets of conversation she imagines having with Rich. These conversations are expansive. They are lived in the friendship of the black woman and the white Jewish woman who share the common bond of being women and lesbians. These identities move them outward, as if friendship were the potential for "another whole structure that touches every aspect of our existence." Rich, too, pulls Lorde into another thought world, opens the possibilities.

IT'S INTRIGUING that one of the few narratives about Israelite friendship also concerns a friendship that crosses ethnic lines. In the book of Ruth we're given the chance to eavesdrop on a friendship bound by common and diverging sources of trauma and hope. We bear witness to a complex relationship, a friendship reaching across the boundaries of ethnicity and biological kinship, and at times, erasing otherness.

Friendship is a fragile gift. Even for Ruth and Naomi the possibilities of friendship are elusive. It proves difficult to wrest friendship from the power of biological kinship and genealogical patriarchy that governs the Old Testament narrative. And so it is that in the end Ruth will be subsumed into marriage, and this marriage will erase her from the text. Just as it was for Tamar, there are no options for a life outside the confines of male protection. There is desperation in the story of the two single women, unprotected in Judah, fending for themselves. At each juncture Ruth repeats her concern about the availability of food. Hunger haunts the pages.

Eventually Ruth and Naomi devise a plan for a more permanent security, working out a plan in which the still-eligible Ruth will unite with a distant relative of Naomi's late husband, a man named Boaz. Once the arrangement is made for the betrothal, Ruth loses her name. To the men who bear witness to the transaction, she is no longer called Ruth but instead is referred to as "the young woman" or "the woman" (Ruth 4:11-12).

As a final reminder of the pervasiveness of heredity, Ruth's firstborn child is taken by Naomi. As the child is placed in his grandmother's arms, Ruth vanishes, her Moabite ethnicity subsumed into the genealogy of King David. The women of the village exclaim that a child has been born not to Ruth but to Naomi (Ruth 4:17).

It's a frustrating end to the story for me, but also a reminder that the gift of friendship is a sliver of glass, a brittle stem. And we also know that something lingers. The momentary spark of friendship for Ruth and Naomi is fanned back to flame generations later, in the life of their offspring, Jesus. It is Jesus who, generations later, is deeply moved by the companionship of friends. This Jesus weeps beside the tomb of Lazarus. (John 11:34-35). He receives the intimate gift of perfume from Mary, and calls Martha "the one he loves" (John 12:3, 11:5). This Jesus reclines next to the beloved disciple at the last supper (John 13:23). He seeks out those close to him to draw near when he is afraid (Matthew 26:38). The root of Naomi and Ruth's friendship blooms in the life of Jesus.

EVEN AS THE BONDS of friendship are frustrated by patriarchal institutions, the book of Ruth is strengthened by one other bond, another witness to the survival of women throughout time. Here, in the final chapters of the book, we meet the "women of the neighborhood" (Ruth 4:17).

God, the one who restores and nourishes life, does so through a community of women who become Naomi's people. At the end, standing around her, the women of the neighborhood pronounce a blessing upon Naomi. These women, not the child's father or mother, name the baby Obed. This is the only occurrence in the Old Testament where a group of women give a child a name.

I don't expect that anything could fill the space in Naomi's heart. Loss is more complicated than that. But I do find the presence of friends in my life opens up space for a reimagined family—that God conceives a way of being bound to one another outside blood ties. There is a stirring and remaking in the midst of tragedy. What emerges is a new kinship, a new belonging, the covenant love between Naomi and Ruth, a child, a neighborhood of women blessing.

The women of the neighborhood find their way to me, offering me their blessing. One week I peered into our play room to see a friend pretending "baby owl" in the corner with my toddler. I could hear their laughter fill the house as I left for work. A few days later, one of the teenagers from my church took my child to the playground during Sunday school. She was pushed into the air on a swing, head back in the wind, mine and ours, a child of our common life in God.

As I watched them from the window, I remembered how for years our daughter's Sunday school class was taught by a single woman from our church. I am mindful of how much of our little one's understanding of God was formed by this foster mother of faith. So many women of the neighborhood are creating bonds of strength and resistance that will sustain her as the full force of the world's terror works its way into her life.

I also know these bonds, and the communities that form through them, do so with risk. Our friendships, our churches, unfold within relationships where we name our difference. And we look towards the places where we erase our difference. I sense the risk when Ruth—her Moabite identity, her female identity—vanishes from the end of the book named in her honor. We must pay attention here, refusing to see Ruth and Naomi as a story of heroic sisterhood and seamless unity. The work of liberation, for ourselves and for others, is to look past these fables of idealized solidarity into the complicated, risky territory of friendship.

But we continue to risk, because to whom else will we go? "To grow in love-ability," writes the philosopher Gillian Rose, "is to accept the boundaries of oneself and others, while remaining vulnerable, woundable, around the bounds."[6] To find our way to friendship, we risk and we hope.

This risk—this self-attention, failure, forgiveness, and willingness to try again—is the form God's action takes in the story of Ruth and Naomi. Renita Weems, in her reflections on this female friendship, writes,

> Notice: In the darkest moments of the story—when Naomi was bereft of her husband and children, when Orpah and Ruth were bereft of their husbands, when the women had to decide whether or not to abandon one another—no angel of mercy came to the women's defense. No divine messenger offered counsel to the bewildered. No God came with words of wisdom and assurance. Naomi, Orpah, and Ruth were left with the integrity of their faith and the strength of their relationship with one another. The women had to make their own decisions.[7]

Weems reminds me of the power of the Old Testament witness that runs the length of the Scriptures, from the creation of the world to the prophets. God's action comes in the form of human involvement, God works hand in hand with human work. The Old Testament is wary of a spiritual life that is not enfleshed in neighbors and war, feasts and want, bathing and fleeing, marriage and farming, death and rest.

A story with flesh and bones. As Christian readers of the Old Testament, we are not objective observers. The story of God's faithful love, interrupted by human disobedience, is written so that each of us becomes a character in it. This story is to be read from the inside out, as we push and pull at the narratives, argue with the characters, demand an answer from our enemies and heroes and even from God.

The Old Testament is a participatory story because, as Willie Jennings reminds Christians, "We joined the story of another people, of Israel, and in this way learned of our God."[8] We enter these stories as the Gentile other—those welcomed into God's promises despite being outsiders.

When Christians read the Old Testament, we do so because an act of grace has found its way to us: God calling us a friend when once we were far from God. The gift of the Old Testament is that it tells us this story over and over again. Once when we were far away God came for us, and loved us, and showed us the way to be free.

Acknowledgments

Many people read or heard these words before they came to print, including my editor, Valerie Weaver-Zercher, as well as Colin Cornell, Erica Littlewolf, Amos Caley, Theresa Thames, Michael McGregor, Ann Hall, Cullen McKenney, my Collegeville Institute writing group, and the people of Raleigh Mennonite Church. To Isaac Villegas, who read all the words—thank you. The time you each gave is a gift to me.

I'm grateful to the Lilly Foundation for numerous supports and resources over the past decade, and to the Collegeville Institute for a place to write, read, pray, and let my words be heard by others.

Thanks to Mary Nilsen, who showed me how to write; Elaine Phillips, who introduced me to the Old Testament; Marv Wilson, who taught me Hebrew; and Ellen Davis, who helped me find God in the Bible. I have been blessed by the most excellent teachers in the classroom and beyond.

I'm grateful to my sister, Heather Bixler, my longest friend. I am grateful for Jacob Florer-Bixler, whose time caring for children in the home has made it possible for me to spend my time writing these words. Over the years many people have made a family out of friendship—Gwyneth Jones, Carla Evans, the Smalleys, Jillaine Baker, Fran Saylor, and Gair McCullough. Thank you. For my dear friends in L'Arche Portland—Joni Smith, Adam Richards, Erin Wheeler, and Marilyn Pettruzelli—thank you for showing me a life of patience and gentleness.

I am wordlessly grateful to my parents, Bill and Robbin Bixler, who throughout my life have revealed to me God's nature of selfless and unconditional love. I love you.

And finally for my children—Tennyson, Wick, and Etta Wren. Every day with you is a gift.

Notes

A PRAYER FOR READERS

1 Images from: Isaiah 42:14 (woman in labor); Genesis 1 (hovering over creation); Isaiah 49:15 (nursing mother); Ezekiel 34:11-16 (searching in fields); Isaiah 5:2-7 (uprooting his garden); Isaiah 7:18 (keeping her bees); Psalm 17:8 (bird in tree); Hosea 14:6 (sprouting tree); Jeremiah 17:13 (rushing fountain); Jeremiah 1:13 (steaming pot); Hosea 13:8 (a raging she-bear); Exodus 19:18 (smoking kiln); Exodus 24:17, Lamentation 2:4, Numbers 11:1, and Deuteronomy 5:24 (fire).

PREFACE

1 Marilynne Robinson, *Lila* (New York: Picador, 2015), 128.

2 Ibid., 82.

3 Rowan Williams, "Living the Good Life: Rowan Williams on Marilynne Robinson," *The New Statesman* (October 16, 2014).

4 Ellen Davis, *Getting Involved with God: Rediscovering the Old Testament* (Lanham: Cowley Publications, 2001), 3.

1. GOD OF RECKONING

1 "Born in Slavery: Slave Narratives from the Federal Writers' Project: 1936-1938," Library of Congress Slave Narrative Project, Vol. 11, North Carolina, Part 1, Adams-Hunter, http://hdl.loc.gov/loc.mss/mesn.111.

2 Malinda Elizabeth Berry, "Milbank, Theology, and Stories of the Marginalized," *Conrad Grebel Review* (Spring 2005), 27.

3 Robert Darden, *People Get Ready! A New History of Black Gospel Music* (New York: Continuum, 2004), 95.

4 Rowan Williams, *Tokens of Trust: An Introduction to Christian Belief* (Louisville: Westminster John Knox, 2007), 17.

5 Daniel Boyarin, *Carnal Israel: Reading Sex in Talmudic Culture* (Berkeley: University of California Press, 1993) https://faculty.georgetown.edu/jod/augustine/ddc.html, accessed Oct 7, 2018.

6 Augustine, *De doctrina christiana*, Preface 6.

7 Lydia Harder, "Hermeneutic Community—A Feminist Challenge," in *Perspectives on Feminist Hermeneutics*, eds. Gayle Koontz and Willard Swartley (Occasional Papers No. 10, Institute on Mennonite Studies).

2. GOD OF NEIGHBORS

1 Wilda C. Gafney, *Womanist Midrash: A Reintroduction to the Women of the Torah and the Throne* (Louisville: Westminster John Knox, 2007), 107–108.

2 Jason Byassee, "How the Church Grew in South Sudan," *Christian Century* (December 2, 2010).

3 Jacob Milgrom, *Leviticus: A Book of Rituals and Ethics* (Minneapolis: Augsburg Press, 2004), xii.

4 Ibid.

5 Gafney, 107.

6 Mary Douglas, *Purity and Danger: An Analysis of Concepts of Pollution and Taboo* (London: Routledge, 1966), 345–49.

7 Martin Buber, *On Judaism* (New York: Schocken, 1967), 212.

8 Milgrom, *Leviticus*, 237.

9 Felipe Hinojosa, *Latino Mennonites: Civil Rights, Faith, and Evangelical Culture* (Baltimore: Johns Hopkins University Press), 59.

10 Vincent Harding, "The Beggars Are Rising: Where Are the Saints?" quoted in Joanna Shenk, *The Movement Makes Us Human: An Interview with Dr. Vincent Harding on Mennonites* (Eugene: Wipf and Stock, 2018)

11 Hinojosa, *Latino Mennonites*, 59.

3. GOD OF VICTIMS

1 Waugh, Irma Morales. "Examining the Sexual Harassment Experiences of Mexican Immigrant Farmworking Women." January 21, 2010, https://www.ncbi.nlm.nih.gov/pubmed/20093433, accessed Sept 15, 2018.

2 Ramchandani, Ariel. "There's a Sexual-Harassment Epidemid on America's Farms" in *The Atlantic*, Jan 29, 2018, https://www.theatlantic.com/business/archive/2018/01/agriculture-sexual-harassment/550109/, accessed Sept 17, 2018

3 *Time* magazine, Time staff, "700,000 Female
   Farmworkers Say They Stand With Hollywood Actors
   Against Sexual Assault," Nov 10, 2017, http://time.
   com/5018813/farmworkers-solidarity-hollywood-sexual-
   assault/, accessed Oct 1, 2018

4 Michelle Alexander, *The New Jim Crow: Mass
   Incarceration in the Age of Colorblindness* (New York:
   The New Press, 2010), 4.

4. GOD OF MEMORY

1 Walter Brueggemann, "Emergent Theological
   Conversation 2004," (christianaudio: March 5, 2006).

2 Leon R. Kass, *The Beginning of Wisdom: Reading
   Genesis* (Chicago: University of Chicago Press, 2006),
   367–68.

5. GOD OF WANDERERS

1 Pope Alexander VI, *The Papal Bull Inter Caetera*,
   1493. See Stephen Newcomb, Pagans In a Promised
   Land: Decoding the Doctrine of Discovery (Fulcrum
   Publishing, 2008)

2 Rowan Williams introduced me to Etty Hillesum in his
   book *Tokens of Trust.*

3 Etty Hillesum, *Etty: The Letters and Diaries of Etty
   Hillesum, 1941-1943* (Grand Rapids: Eerdmans, 2002).

4 Ibid, 468.

6. GOD OF DARKNESS

1 Virginia Woolf, *The Letters of Virginia Woolf: Volume II,
   1912–1922*, ed. Nigel Nicolson and Joanne Trautmann
   (New York: Harcourt Brace Jovanovich, 1976), 585.

2 Barbara Brown Taylor, *Learning to Walk in the Dark* (New York: HarperCollins, 2014), 146.

7. GOD OF WONDER

1 *Mishnah Bikkurim* 1.3, https://www.sefaria.org/Mishnah_Bikkurim?lang=bi, accessed Feb 4, 2018.

2 Dorothy Day, *The Long Loneliness: The Autobiography of Dorothy Day* (New York: Harper & Brothers Publishers, 1952).

3 Kate DiCamillo, *Flora and Ulysses* (Candlewick Press, 2013), graphic novel, chapter 21.

8. GOD OF BIRDS

1 Mary Oliver, *Our Life* (Boston: Beacon Press, 2009).

9. GOD OF THE VULNERABLE

1 *Berakhot* 55b, https://www.sefaria.org/Berakhot.55b?lang=bi, accessed Feb 15, 2018.

2 Tertullian, *On the Flesh of Christ*, 5 (Savage MN: Lighthouse Christian Publishing, 2015).

3 Anne-Sophie Constant, Jean Vanier: *Portrait of a Free Man* (Walden, NY: Plough Publishing House, 2019).

4 Jean Vanier, *Our Life Together: A Memoir in Letters* (London: Darton Longman Todd, 2008), Letter August 22, 1964, 15.

5 Jean Vanier, *Community and Growth* (Mahwah, NJ: Paulist Press, 1989), 43.

6 Ibid.

10. GOD OF THE TABLE

1 Gregory Nazianzus, *Orations* 40.41. (Gregory Nazianzus, *Orations* 40.41.), accessed March 22, 2018.

2 Menno Simmons, "Foundations of Christian Doctrine" in *The Complete Writings of Menno Simmons* (Scottdale: Herald Press, 1956).

11. GOD OF FRIENDSHIP

1 Peter Dula, *Cavell, Companionship, and Christian Theology* (New York: Oxford University Press, 2011), 112.

2 Leon Kass, *The Beginning of Wisdom,* (Chicago: University of Chicago Press: 2006), 526-533.

3 Ibid., 532.

4 Paul J. Wadell, *Friendship and the Moral Life* (South Bend, IN: University of Notre Dame Press, 1989), 145–46.

5 Audre Lorde, *Sister Outsider: Essays and Speeches* (Berkeley: Crossing Press, 1984), 94.

6 Gillian Rose, *Love's Work: A Reckoning with Life* (New York: Schocken, 1996), 105.

7 Renita J. Weems, *Just a Sister Away: Understanding the Timeless Connection Between Women of Today and Women in the Bible* (New York: Warner Books Edition, 2005), Chapter 2, page 29.

8 Willie Jennings, "Overcoming Racial Faith," *Duke Divinity Magazine* (Spring 2015), 8.

The Author

Melissa Florer-Bixler is the pastor of Raleigh Mennonite Church in North Carolina. She holds an MA in religion from Duke University and an MDiv from Princeton Theological Seminary. Her writing can be found in *Christian Century*, *Faith & Leadership*, *Mennonite World Review*, *Anabaptist Witness*, *Vision*, *The Salt Collective*, *The Mennonite*, and *Geez Magazine*. Her ministry has been featured in *Sojourners* and *The Atlantic*. Melissa serves on the board of L'Arche North Carolina, a community for people with and without intellectual disabilities. She serves on the Raleigh Human Relations Commission, the strategy team for broad-based organizing in Wake County, and the Equity Committee of her children's school.